THE
JOHN DEERE
WAY

THE
JOHN DEERE
WAY

Performance That Endures

David Magee

WILEY

John Wiley & Sons, Inc.

Published by John Wiley & Sons, Inc., Hoboken, New Jersey.
Published simultaneously in Canada.

For general information on our other products and services please contact our Customer Care Department within the United States at (800) 762-2974, outside the United States at (317) 572-3993 or fax (317) 572-4002.

Designations used by companies to distinguish their products are often claimed by trademarks. In all instances where the author or publisher is aware of a claim, the product names appear in Initial Capital letters. Readers, however, should contact the appropriate companies for more complete information regarding trademarks and registration.

Wiley also publishes its books in a variety of electronic formats. Some content that appears in print may not be available in electronic books. For more information about Wiley products, visit our web site at www.wiley.com.

Library of Congress Cataloging-in-Publication Data:
Magee, David, 1965–
    The John Deere way : performance that endures / David Magee.
      p.   cm.
    Includes bibliographical references.
    ISBN 0-471-70644-2 (cloth)
   1. Deere & Company—History. 2. Deere, John, 1804–1886. 3. Agricultural machinery industry—United States—History. I. Title.
    HD9486.U6D436 2005
    338.7'6313'0973—dc22

                                             2004028739

Printed in the United States of America.

10 9 8 7 6 5 4 3 2 1

For the farmer

Contents

Great companies have a sense of purpose that goes deeper than the bottom line.

> —Hans Becherer, former Chairman and CEO (1989–2000), Deere & Company

We are striving to build a great business. What's most important is how we do it.

> —Robert W. (Bob) Lane, Chairman and CEO, Deere & Company

Prologue

WHEN MY EDITOR AND I WENT IN SEARCH OF AMERICA'S
most values-based business to illustrate the current trend in
today's corporate world, it did not take long to narrow a short
list down to one. John Deere is a global company rooted in
the Midwest that has based its business on principles instilled over time beginning with the day in 1837 when blacksmith John Deere invented the self-scouring steel plow.
John Deere's plow led to a dramatic change in the efficiency
of western agriculture and was the backbone of the company he developed, which has evolved over more than a
century and a half into a world leader in products related to
the land.

I had general knowledge of John Deere and its core agricultural and consumer equipment lines long before arriving
on the scene to try to crack the secrets to success of this enduring company. I knew that many farmers have through
the years relied on John Deere tractors, combines, and attachments with passion and unwavering trust. I knew that
some doctors, lawyers, and businessmen loved bush-hogging
on weekend farms with their beloved John Deere tractor

more than they loved golf, tennis, or hunting. I knew that
John Deere stood behind products with a brand promise of
high quality. And I knew that many lifelong collectors liked
to migrate closer to any of the trademark green and yellow
John Deere products because of the company's unique heritage and distinct characteristics.

What I did not fully understand is the deep level of passion for John Deere, including its products and brand, that
runs all over the world among the widest variety of individuals, including some whose families have been directly involved with the company or its products for generations and
others who have never touched, much less ridden, green John
Deere equipment labeled with the famous yellow logo. More
than just a leading manufacturer of agricultural products,
John Deere, through its unwavering commitment to the land
and the people who work it, has evolved over decades into a
mainstream cultural icon of value and endurance.

Adored by everyone from tough men to trendy fashion-
istas, the John Deere brand today is one of the strongest in
America and many other parts of the world. Farmers involved in the fast-developing agricultural industry in Brazil
embrace John Deere tractors and harvesting equipment,
while celebrities including actor Ashton Kutcher and tennis star Andy Roddick frequently wear John Deere trucker
caps in public appearances. From the popular hats
adorned with the John Deere logo, to riding lawn mowers,
to high-end crop harvesters, John Deere is worn, ridden,
and used every day from Moline to Manhattan and from

Germany to Brazil, its brand represented by the trademark image of the yellow deer leaping on a green background and the widely-recognized advertising slogan Nothing Runs Like a Deere.

Tractor and farm equipment is still the largest part of John Deere sales. The Moline, Illinois–based Fortune 500 company is still agricultural and rural at heart, but has been expanding the breadth of its brand for more than 30 years into such areas as consumer lawn products, landscape, turf management, health care, commercial construction, and forestry equipment. John Deere's close alliance with the global farming community and the company's brand diversification have allowed John Deere to grow in recent years despite continued contraction and massive realignment of the North American agricultural industry.

Under the leadership of chairman and CEO Robert W. (Bob) Lane, John Deere is today doing $20 billion in annual sales with 46,000 employees and has sold products in 160 countries. Included under the John Deere umbrella are equipment lines for agriculture, forestry, construction, lawn and turf care, and golf course maintenance, as well as credit and managed health care services and engine manufacturing. Licensing is also becoming a business of its own, as the John Deere brand stands stronger in its 168th year of business than ever before, and people from around the world reach to identify with this symbol of rural toughness. One can now buy John Deere boots, a John Deere bicycle, or a popular video game (*John Deere: American Farmer*) among literally hundreds of items distinguished by the John Deere corporate brand mark.

But some things have not changed. The company is still rooted in its independent dealer base, serving customers including farmers, builders, and consumers community by community. Many of the John Deere dealers run businesses that have been passed down from generation to generation, and many customer families have followed the progressive path with them, experiencing the company's changing products along the way, from the original steel plow to the two-cylinder Model D tractor first launched in 1924 to today's highly-productive, $250,000 9750 STS combine. And the heart of the company is still the values that have been passed along as lore from Moline to operations around the world year after year.

For example, it is not uncommon for employees today to quote with a straight face company founder John Deere when making a point. *What would John Deere have done?* Simply, the company that began in 1837 when the blacksmith first helped farmers cut through sticky Midwest soil with the invention of his self-scouring plow is still practicing the same values its founder preached, albeit under contemporary leadership, vision, and new objectives. Bob Lane, for example, has led a charge of almost five years to apply John Deere's principles to the business side of the equation in an effort to make the company one that performs at a high level in all aspects year after year.

John Deere has not been a perfect company during its more than a century and a half in business, and certainly mistakes have been made. But the lessons learned along the way in good times and bad have only served to strengthen the foundation of the company that strives on a daily basis to deliver Performance That Endures to customers, employees, and shareholders. The secrets to the success of John Deere are the premise of this work, a primer for the everyman who aspires to the same qualities that have served the company well for decades, the qualities that come together to create The John Deere Way.

Introduction

WHEN DAVID MAGEE FIRST APPROACHED JOHN DEERE WITH his idea for a book on the company, we were honored to be considered worthy of the time and effort an author must invest to learn about an organization and to tell its story. We agreed to let David have access to employees, retirees, our archives, and our meetings because we thought perhaps he was right, that there might be a story to tell, and because we were curious to see how an outside, independent author would assess the company. David has been persistent as well as enthusiastic in his search to define what has made the company and its products such a unique part of the lives of so many, for so many years. He went in search of the secrets to this success and came away in the end defining what he now calls "The John Deere Way."

For many, much of what you will find inside is second nature wherever you do your job every day. John Deere has been based since its founding on dedicated employees who understand, foster, and nurture the important qualities that make John Deere a company we are all privileged to be a part of. For us, however, it is useful to see and learn what this author discovered in his yearlong endeavor to find and reveal the key elements to John Deere's enduring success.

Much has been written about John Deere through the years, and these valuable works help us to understand and appreciate the vital role this global company and its products have played for decades. Here, however, David takes a different approach, writing about the business practices and attitudes that created John Deere as we know it today as well as analyzing the actions and efforts that will build our future. We find his assessment to be insightful and, though we have never articulated it in this manner, aligned with what we see as the foundation of the company's enduring success.

By reading this book, you'll discover what might seem intuitive and simple, and perhaps, at first blush, you'll come away thinking there must be something more. How can a global company with such far-reaching and ambitious products and services thrive under some very basic principles of business and trust? Yet, as David has discerned, it is easy to talk about values such as commitment and integrity. It is much more difficult to instill into a company so completely a core set of values that they become the foundation of long-term success worldwide. How this has occurred and what exactly these values mean to the company, including its customers, employees, shareholders, suppliers, and dealers, is the revealed strength of this project. Understanding the seemingly simple qualities that make John Deere unique is to understand how we provide solutions to complex challenges around the world.

At John Deere, we are keenly interested in *how* we do business, and we hold true to our core values. Values of integrity, quality, innovation, and commitment are never to be compromised. We are dedicated to living our values and, through doing so, growing a business as great as our products. By doing so, we continue to enhance the legacy that we have inherited from strong leaders and loyal employees, passing along an even stronger legacy to the future.

Deere people throughout the world are unparalleled in their skill and unmatched in their passion and enthusiasm. Our dealers are consistently cited as one of the main reasons customers buy quality John Deere products, parts, and service. Our suppliers are superior at delivering on time and on spec. And all of this effort is supported by an across-the-board strong heritage of quality and integrity.

Throughout our history, John Deere has earned a reputation for high quality and integrity, and this has been an asset of incalculable value. We strive to live up to these expectations, not just because it is good business, but because it is the right thing to do. Integrity is never to be compromised for immediate success. Rather, integrity is viewed as a long-term proposition for all with whom the company is involved.

We can trace our company's commitment to integrity to our founder, John Deere. In 1837 Deere, a transplanted Vermont blacksmith, was inspired to forge a special plow from a discarded saw blade, and in doing so allowed farmers to till the sticky soil of the American Great Plains. While his plows helped prepare the soil for the sowing of crops for Midwestern settlers, Deere began to build a company that would live up to the phrase attributed to him: "I will not put my name on a product that does not have in it the best that is in me." To this we still aspire.

Of course, customers determine when we are great. A great business serves their needs. All product offerings and supporting activities are to meet their standards of high quality and value. So, all involved—our employees, our dealers, and our suppliers—work to be first and to earn sustained preeminence in the eyes of our customers.

Today, we are targeting everyday performance to be on average better than ever before. Our goal, in short, is to build a business, and an investment, worthy of the quality products we make and the uncommonly dedicated people around the world who make them. Our current actions set the tone for how a lean, well-disciplined enterprise—where all are committed to great products, profitable growth, and world-class capital efficiency—should do business. It's the kind of global performance company we're determined to become.

When we say performance, we mean performance that endures. It's the kind of thing that can be achieved only by a great company with exceptional employees, dealers, and suppliers operating as a great business, producing superior products and services with the advanced technology customers want and need. We're confident John Deere is well on the way to creating a new level of financial and operating excellence.

While this book is a fitting tribute to the employees and

leaders of John Deere who have built and nurtured this company in the past with commitment, integrity, innovation, and quality, it also identifies why we at John Deere today believe that our best days—days of sustained high performance—are in the future.

David's insights into the essence of John Deere are fascinating, and I hope you find his observations of benefit to your own personal or business life.

Robert W. Lane
Chairman and CEO
Deere & Company

CHAPTER
ONE

Embrace the Culture

A DISTINGUISHING CHARACTERISTIC OF GREAT COMPANIES IS almost always a unique culture that may evolve over time but that remains true to the people who continually get the job done. At John Deere, understanding the corporate culture is to understand how the company that started out making single-furrow farm plows in the Midwest 168 years ago has managed to grow into a global company with diverse products and services recognized by customers and admirers as a symbol of reliability, trust, and value.

At its heart, John Deere's culture is rooted in the land and is reflected in employees through the values of those who work the land, resulting in a dominant theme of *how* business is done, which begins with the company's top leadership and runs throughout. At John Deere, *how* the job gets done is more important than simply getting it done. Whether it involves designing, manufacturing, selling, serving top of the line agricultural, forestry, or construction equipment, or lawn and turf care equipment, or processing a credit application, John Deere employees know that the primary litmus test for decision making and action should be based on such factors as telling the truth, treating others with fairness, and standing behind the company's products and services.

This do-it-right philosophy began with company founder John Deere and has endured through the years, even though generations of employees have come and gone, because of a variety of factors, most notably a strong foundation, continuity in leadership, and Midwestern heritage. The *how* is based upon four basic tenets of doing business that are applied in every division at every level in all decision making: quality, innovation, integrity, and commitment—values that company founder John Deere lived by and instilled into the company from the day in 1837 that the 33-year-old first started selling his steel, self-scouring plow to solve a customer need for better equipment.

THE RIGHT PRODUCT AT THE RIGHT TIME

A native of Vermont, John Deere had migrated in 1836 to Grand Detour, Illinois, a frontier settlement in the northwestern portion of the state. An accomplished blacksmith, Deere, whose business in Vermont had been struggling, was seeking new business opportunity in the developing region. Deere's blacksmith shop grew as he crafted a range of products from hayforks to horseshoes and metal parts for wagons and stagecoaches. He was curiously intrigued, however, by what area farmers told him about their problems tilling the dense, rich Midwestern soil. The dirt caked on farmers' cast-iron plows, making the work day slow, laborious, and often unprofitable because so much time had to be spent cleaning mud from plows.

Deere talked to farmers and researched the problem by studying what plows were available in the marketplace. Dozens of companies were selling thousands of plows at the time, but most were made in the Northeast, where understanding of problems plaguing the Midwest farmer was limited. The plows were all essentially the same. John Deere determined that the best means to get through the sticky Midwest soil was a plow that scoured the land, letting dirt slide off it. In 1837, he took a broken steel sawmill blade, curved it, and designed the self-scouring steel plow, dramatically improving farm efficiency.

Over the next several years, Deere's blacksmith business evolved into primarily an agricultural equipment manufacturing trade as word of his plows spread among area farmers. It did not happen fast. Deere sold just 10 plows in 1839, 40 in 1840, and 75 in 1841, while other plow manufacturers in the United States were selling thousands during the same period, dwarfing his tiny operation. But Deere's ingenuity, craftsmanship, and attention to detail brought him growing attention and customers in his region. For while the plow was the right product at the right time and earned him a permanent place in American agricultural history, Deere's greatest contribution to today's John Deere may be the values he instilled into the company from the start and backed up until his death in 1886 in Moline, Illinois.

Known as "an intense and thorough" man, John Deere was a product of his times, part of the developing, rough, American frontier, and his charismatic personality was colored by a gruff, sometimes undiplomatic manner. But he was consistent in the tenets of business he preached throughout his 22 years at the helm of the company, insisting it never stray from the four core values he believed mattered most: quality, innovation, integrity, and commitment. And he personified the very values he spoke of, subscribing to a theory that if he could better himself, it was his responsibility to bring others along with him, and as a result he treated his employees and customers fairly. Deere was also a staunch abolitionist before and during the Civil War, speaking out publicly without fear of damage to his business because of his desire to end slavery.

CONTINUITY OF LEADERSHIP

A primary reason John Deere's influence remains strong today among 46,000 employees in the company bearing his name is that even though it was 168 years ago when he invented the self-scouring plow, only seven other chief executive officers have served the company (see Appendix A) since he retired in 1859 to make way for his son, Charles Deere. One would expect John Deere to have had a minimum of 15 leaders, or perhaps as many as 25, during its two-century span of business. Remarkably, the total number is only eight over the entire John Deere corporate history, including five members of the Deere family.

Thus, John Deere's continuity of leadership has allowed the company's vision to remain connected to founding values over the duration of time. Because while each of John Deere's eight chief officers tackled broad, independent initiatives deemed best for the company at the time, all took or are taking the principles instilled by the founder from the moment they accepted the charge, and passed or are passing them along to generation after generation of Deere employees. The leaders were and are focused on John Deere's values instead of grasping at a variety of passing, outside business trends, and they built and are building on strengths and weaknesses of their predecessors in building block fashion. As a result, the John Deere culture has been additive over time, the core values remaining as the anchor.

> *I believe all of our present strengths have been built on the foundation of achievement, integrity, and momentum that we have inherited from our predecessors.*
> —Robert A. Hanson, John Deere CEO, 1982–1989

John Deere's college-educated son, Charles Deere, took over leadership of the agricultural equipment maker in 1859 at the age of 21, bringing to the company a more formal approach than his father to business development and growth. Charles Deere ran the company for 49 years, leading John

Deere to tremendous growth during his tenure, including an increase in sales from $200,000 to $3 million. Under his leadership the company underwent such changes as formal incorporation in the name of Deere & Company from its previous trade name of Moline Plow Manufactory to the opening of the company's first branch houses (Deere, Mansur & Co. opened in Kansas City, Missouri, in 1869 to sell products within a certain geographic area), resulting in organizational decentralization that strongly impacts the way John Deere is run today.

The five branches Charles Deere had established by 1889 from Kansas City to San Francisco were set up as entities separate from Deere & Company but were under the umbrella of its name and products. Each of the branches, with different owners partnering with Deere and entrepreneurial incentive, developed individual means of selling product and working with customers. But each also worked closely with Deere & Company in Moline in regard to product development and sharing information from the field with company headquarters.

Still today, Charles Deere's influence remains strong in the company since John Deere employees around the world are empowered to make decisions to get the job done through a decentralized system and culture that honors the abilities of employees—as long as they adhere to the spirit of long-standing core values. In other words, they are accountable and are expected to communicate actions and results, but if they are striving to meet set objectives and to follow the laid out tenets of *how*, they can get the job done by making swift, effective decisions at the source of the problem or action.

When Charles Deere died in 1907, he was succeeded by his son-in-law, William Butterworth (married to Katherine Deere). A lawyer by training, Butterworth was a conservative businessman who stressed loyalty, trust, and service to John Deere employees and it was during his tenure that the company consolidated into its modern corporate form, including the centralization of accounting and financial planning. In essence, he created an umbrella for John Deere best described as a hub and spoke system of manufacturing and distribution. It was also under Butterworth that John Deere made the important move into the tractor manufacturing business in 1918 when the company purchased the Waterloo Boy tractor company, a shifting moment in corporate history.

When Butterworth retired in 1928 to head the U.S. Chamber of Commerce, he turned over leadership of the company to John Deere's great-grandson, Charles Deere Wiman. Under Wiman's leadership, the size of the company increased from $64 million to $340 million as he emphasized efficient production and engineering and John Deere's reliable two-cylinder tractor became a staple of the American farm. Perhaps most importantly, when the nation suffered under the Great Depression and World War II during his leadership, Wiman's ability to recognize and reward the integrity of individuals led John Deere to compassionate acts during the difficult times.

THE MODERN DAY FATHER OF THE COMPANY

William (Bill) Hewitt, the last member of the Deere family to run the company, is arguably the modern day father of the company due to his unprecedented foresight in blending design, style, and global reflections with John Deere's rural, Midwestern heritage. This combination of refined sophistication and farm toughness was a catalyst in elevating John Deere to preeminent status as a global brand, beginning in the 1960s and an originating point for today's cultural movement toward urban toughness. The son-in-law of Charles Deere Wiman, Hewitt had a taste for art, fine wine, and design and began integrating elements of this taste into John Deere and its products early in his 27-year tenure, which began in 1955.

It was during the Hewitt period that John Deere began a transformation in the eyes of customers into a more contemporary, exuberant brand that stood above others, not only in quality, but also in style. Additionally, Hewitt had a warm appreciation of Deere leaders and employees who had served before him and often quoted past stories of conservative wisdom and leadership to fellow workers as a means of making a point and reinforcing the values-based culture while adding a flavor of global confidence and tastes. By the time he retired in 1982 (serving an appointment as U.S. ambassador to Jamaica and then moving to the Napa Valley), John Deere was the world's leading manufacturer of farm equipment, and its products stood out among competitors for value, style, and longevity.

VALUES ARE THE STRENGTH FOR SURVIVING TOUGH TIMES

The first non-family member to become chief executive at John Deere was Robert A. (Bob) Hanson, who took over after Bill Hewitt in 1982, 145 years after John Deere had founded the company. Times could not have been tougher, as the American farming boom in the decade of the 1970s gave way to a painful economic recession in the early 1980s—coinciding with Hanson's tenure. As good as the 1970s had been for agriculture companies, when advances in production had led to record yields, which had combined with increased export demand to create the perfect supply and demand scenario, the 1980s were equally bad. In 1980, for instance, one year after U.S. agricultural equipment sales were at an all-time high, President Jimmy Carter imposed an embargo on grain sales to the Soviet Union, reducing demand and sending prices on a downward spiral. Farmers could no longer pay for equipment purchased during the expansion, and prices for farm land and commodities dropped considerably. Farm equipment manufacturers suffered greatly. John Deere lost $229 million in 1986—its first loss in 53 years—and another $190 million in 1987. A native of Moline and a former boxer, Hanson's fighting spirit and leadership helped the company emerge from the recession in better shape than its competitors did. John Deere continued investing in product and actually increased sales by more than $2.5 billion during Hanson's tenure.

In fact, as difficult as the 1980s were for John Deere, history shows the period to be an important time in the company's evolving business history, since many necessary business reforms were put in place that would be useful later. Additionally, hiring was essentially frozen for almost a decade and thousands were laid off. At the peak of America's roaring farm days in 1979, for example, John Deere had had 65,000 employees, but that number dropped by more than half 15 years later (31,500). The upside is that John Deere's culture remained strong at its 150-year anniversary because the employees who had remained during the contraction were among the most experienced and ingrained in John Deere's values-based culture. A sort of selective reduction resulted as the stronger employees—the ones most understanding and committed to the John Deere way—had survived the downsizing, reinforcing the company-wide adherence to quality, innovation, integrity, and commitment.

John Deere's "Genuine Value" program helped the company emerge from the difficult recession as a more lean and diversified manufacturer. The program was led by Hans Becherer, who was president of Deere in 1987 and later took charge as chairman and CEO in 1989. Becherer used Genuine Value as the platform to cut costs across the board, reduce high inventories, and strengthen operating units as decentralized businesses supported by corporate staff departments so that individual businesses could grow, thrive, and profit independently.

The commitment to our values has earned the respect of our customers in the past, and guarantees the success of our business in the future.

—Hans W. Becherer

The son of German immigrants, Becherer grew up in Detroit, graduated from Harvard Business School, did post-graduate work at Munich University while serving in the Air Force in West Germany, and married Michelle, a native of France, in 1959. He joined John Deere in 1966 because of its commitment to his own values and because the company was embarking on global expansion. But when he announced to Harvard classmates that he was moving after graduation to the Midwest to work for a tractor maker, many snickered. It was his lowest-paying offer, and he was by all accounts a city boy with little knowledge about the farms and fields of America.

"I wanted to join a company that was embarking on international growth, one where I could make a difference, and one that was unusual and different," Becherer said. "It was the right decision, because I can't ever remember somebody at John Deere asking me to do something in the name of the company that I did not feel was right."

Becherer led John Deere to almost double sales and to earn $1 billion in profits for the first time ever by pushing the company to diversify through worldwide expansion and product growth, in addition to achieving key reforms following farming's severe contraction during the 1980s. But as Becherer's planned retirement in 2000 neared, the agricultural industry was entering another recession. Direction of leadership at John Deere was critical considering the volatility of the times in American business. Speculation about his successor was widespread inside the company and outside, since for probably the first time in the company's history, the impending direction of leadership was not obvious. John

Deere had several well-qualified insiders capable of leading the company into the new century of business, but none was clearly earmarked to continue the short line of John Deere leadership that had begun with its founder in 1837.

Becherer instituted an informal contest among his leading replacement contenders, assigning each a different leadership position to assess their skills in various environments. Among these high potentials was Robert W. (Bob) Lane, who was promoted first to chief financial officer (CFO) in 1997 and then to senior vice president of Europe, the Middle East, and Africa in 1998.

Working closely with the board of directors, but ultimately making the final decision, Becherer chose Lane as his replacement as chairman and chief executive officer. This decision was made, Becherer said, primarily because he knew that Bob Lane deeply lived and practiced the values preached as core to the success of John Deere. Lane was named CEO in May 2000 and chairman of the board in August 2000, moves Becherer said he considered among his most important acts at Deere because it provided continuity of values-based leadership at the company.

Many corporations, Becherer said, use the wrong criteria when forming a leadership succession plan, but he and the Deere & Company board of directors wanted a person who would sustain the company's values and culture while seeking new opportunities to improve the business. In making his decision, Becherer never got personally close to any candidates so friendship would not be a factor in the decision.

"I enjoyed them all," he said, "and would have had friendships with them, but I never let myself get personally close because to get the right leader, it can't be a personal choice. A lot of companies fail in this . . . it's easy to fail. Bob Lane's qualities of leadership were a great fit to continue the legacy of John Deere."

Once the decision had been made, Becherer worked closely with Lane to ensure the smooth transition that had become part of John Deere's leadership history. Lane was named president of the company and moved into the office next to the chairman's so they could prepare for the change. One incident is remembered as symbolic of how John Deere leadership has cordially handled transition in the top job, adopting ideas of the new leader while maintaining the core values of generations. Hans Becherer, despite his personal objection, agreed to change the dress code at John Deere's world headquarters from "business attire" to "smart dress" — a term Lane used to describe an environment in which employees dress in business casual at the office on days when specific meetings don't dictate otherwise.

Becherer is a business formalist and was not fond of the American corporate movement toward casual dress in the late 1990s. Lane, however, believed the change was important for John Deere to better reflect changing corporate times and to help with company recruitment. He did not, however, believe the change should occur with the changing of the leadership so it would not appear to company employees that it had anything to do with Lane's personal preference. Despite his own preference for more formal business attire, Becherer announced the "smart dress" change while he was still in office to help his successor's transition to office.

"There has always," Becherer said, "been this sort of

ethos handoff from one [leader] to the other. This company is bigger than all of us. We just want to effectively pass it from one generation to the next."

A PATH TO THE FUTURE

Born in Washington, D.C., on November 14, 1949, Lane had graduated with high honors from Wheaton College in Wheaton, Illinois, in 1972 before earning an MBA degree from the University of Chicago in 1974 and then entering banking at First National Bank of Chicago. A rower in high school and a member of the varsity swim team in college, Lane met his wife, Patty, at Wheaton. They married, and were transferred to West Germany by the bank in the late 1970s.

Despite the fact that he had once competed in a collegiate swim meet at Augustana College of Rock Island, Illinois (which adjoins Moline and is one of the Quad Cities), Lane was not familiar with John Deere until he was a senior in college. Ironically, his wife is from Moline and one of his first John Deere experiences was while visiting her home, when he was driven around as a tourist and was shown the company headquarters on an area sightseeing trip. But his first real experiences came as a banker. John Deere was a customer of his through the First National Bank of Chicago and it was through this relationship that he began to learn the values of the company and the strength of its brand. The owner of a large John Deere dealership, in fact, remembers a young Bob Lane calling on him years ago, hoping to get his business. Jerry Swanson, owner of Stribling Equipment, a con-

struction equipment dealer based in the South, said Lane
flew down to Jackson, Mississippi, asked for his business, and
promised to deliver quality and service worthy of John Deere.

In West Germany, Lane was on a leadership track with
the Chicago-based bank and enjoyed finance but was intrigued enough when the opportunity came to interview
with John Deere that he agreed to a meeting. Bob and Patty
Lane drove from Chicago to Moline for an interview at John
Deere in November 1981. They received tickets to hear the
Chicago Symphony—it was Bob's birthday—and went on a
Friday night, before making the three-hour drive west to
Moline for an early Saturday morning interview. The performance, he remembered, was world class. John Deere, he
thought on the drive to Moline the next day, represented the
same thing. Lane believed the uniqueness of John Deere
made the opening a rare, global opportunity.

Lane and his family moved from West Germany to Moline, and he went to work in the finance department of the
construction and equipment division in 1982. "I knew," said
Lane, "that John Deere had all the attributes of the best in
the world at what it does. I loved my job (in banking), but
felt this was a stronger horse, a world-class company. So I
came to this small town to be more global."

With their three children, the Lanes were soon transferred to Denver, Colorado, for five years. After that, they
lived in the Moline area until they were sent back to West
Germany, this time with John Deere. Lane's career took a decided turn toward a faster track overseas, though he did not
consider for many years that a top position was in his future
at John Deere. Lane served as president and chief operating

officer (COO) of John Deere Credit, as chief financial officer of Deere & Company, and as senior vice president and
president of worldwide agricultural equipment, and had led
operations around the world before being told by Becherer
he would succeed the chairman and CEO in 2000.

John Lawson worked at the company for more than 40
years before retiring as a senior vice president in 2001. He
remembers that Bob Lane was not among those first thought
to be in line for succession to the top job. "Bob came out of
the woodwork. But he definitely had the right core values to
lead this great company."

Lane also had an important familial heritage with agriculture, though no one knew it at the time. It relates to Bob
Lane's distant relative John Lane, a third cousin, five times
removed. Historians now believe it was John Lane who actually invented the first steel plow in the 1800s. Deere &
Company has stated for years that John Deere was not the
first maker of a steel plow but was the first to make the steel
plow commercially successful. Also, Lane's plow was much
different from Deere's.

Born in 1793, John Lane was a blacksmith on the north
edge of town in Homer Township, Illinois. In the early
1830s, farmers kept asking Lane if he could improve on the
old wooden plows they had brought from the eastern United
States during their migration to the Midwest. Lane experi-
mented in his shop with flexible steel he had obtained from
a sawmill from old, worn out saw blades. An acquaintance of
Lane's mounted the steel on a wooden frame, and a farmer
in Homer Township used the plow, pulling it through the

thick Illinois sod with from five to eight oxen. Lane began a plow manufacturing business, moving it to nearby Lockport.

In the 1850s he formed a partnership and advertised "Lane's Cast Steel Plows" for sale. Lane did not patent his invention, however, and was said to be willing to share his work with "friends of the soil." John Deere was more successful commercially with the steel plow, obtaining a patent for his unique design while creating a company that is today the world's leading manufacturer of agricultural equipment—headed by Lane's distant cousin. Bob Lane finds humor in the story, and has joked that he came back to claim his family's invention, which is commemorated with a marker placed at the northeast corner of Gougar Road and 7th Street in Homer Township, Illinois, which reads: "In memory of John Lane who made the first steel plow in 1833 on this farm."

Lane muses that his family was not as enterprising as the Deere family and is thankful the patent rests with John Deere, who launched a company that has for 168 years served millions of customers around the world. He knows his challenge is to fortify John Deere's unmatched and integral heritage among employees, while adding new layers that will strengthen the business for the future. When welcoming guests into his office on the second floor of John Deere's Moline, Illinois, headquarters, Lane immediately ushers them into the company's boardroom for a short lesson in history before settling down to business. He stands in the middle of the room, pointing toward an oil painting of the founder, John Deere, and tells about how he founded the company on its core principles.

The wall is covered with portraits of each of John Deere's retired leaders, and Lane pauses at each, noting what the company accomplished during his tenure and making it apparent how each made a sort of ethos handoff to the next. John Deere, he said, is tethered to its past, but constantly striving to go forward. Only by understanding what was previously accomplished and how it was done can one determine needs for the future.

When Lane took over, some things were well established in John Deere's past. The company always had great products. It had already expanded far beyond its original North American territory. And its core values were still intact. Sure, products must always be improved, plenty of areas remained that were ripe for expansion, and values should never be taken for granted. But for a company to move forward and to be firmly established as a great, enduring company, it must continue to improve on its strengths, while striving to add new layers on top of its foundation.

So Lane launched a new initiative after taking office, intended to become the signature of this era of leadership, building on the strengths of those before him. Continuing to be mindful of *how* it is done, John Deere's mission under Lane became squarely focused on building a business as great as the company's products.

CONTINUITY OF THE WORKFORCE

Not only has John Deere experienced stability and low turnover in its executive ranks during its history, but the company has been anchored by a workforce that has been one of the most reliable in the world among major corporations for its longevity and consistency. In 2000, production employees at John Deere had been with the company an average of 22 years, while the national industrial average for similar jobs was 9 years, and the industry average for farm equipment manufacturing and construction equipment manufacturing was 4.9 years and 10.4 years. Simply, despite both global expansion and more broad-based hiring, John Deere still retains employees far longer than most other American companies, as evidenced by half the workforce having 20 years or more with the company.

On production lines, whether in the tractor plant at Waterloo, Iowa, or John Deere Harvester Works, East Moline, Illinois, workers have for generations passed down company lore to one another, reflecting core values and an ongoing commitment to quality. New employees learned from older, more experienced employees through stories and workplace examples, just as parents teach children in homes. It's the same way in corporate offices, where walking the hallways of John Deere's headquarters facility in Moline, it quickly becomes evident that most everybody knows most everybody else, regardless of their employment level, since most have worked together for so many years. Many have been around so long they can recall many specifics about fellow employees' lives, even though they may not be the closest of friends.

So common are 30-year careers at John Deere that employees with less than 20 years' service often still refer to themselves as "newcomers." They feel the need to explain to outsiders why they joined the company in mid-career. And when employees take early retirement, fellow employees sometimes don't understand why they would leave so soon. Mike Orr is a good example. He began work at the company in 1974 for then-chairman and CEO Bill Hewitt after briefly teaching in college and working at a bank.

Orr retired as senior vice president in 2003 after 29 years of service to devote more time to community and charitable causes. He had led the financial services division before retirement and had served four of John Deere's eight chief executives in his 29 years. Still, the company's culture geared toward longevity is so great that colleagues still ribbed him about taking *early* retirement when he departed.

"You read in the business press that long-term commitment is changing," Orr said. "At John Deere, long-term commitment is a reality, so even after 29 years, I was explaining to people why I was leaving so early. Some did not understand."

John Deere's service record among employees has meant that whenever spots needed to be filled at higher levels, plenty of experience has been on hand to choose from, enabling the company to frequently reward from within. This further fosters the culture that John Deere's workforce has always remained close to its founding principles since most managers developed through the same, long apprenticeship system. Additionally, the leadership-from-within style limited the necessity of hiring masses of newcomers at the top who might not understand the intricacies of the farm and equipment business.

"The agricultural business itself is so unique," Orr said. "It is one that the general population itself does not understand. It can also take years of experience to understand

Deere's customer and dealer base and the commitment the company has made to people over the years. There is a better chance of success in picking someone who has this frame of reference as opposed to bringing in someone who's been successful in another business. You can't assume they'll thrive in this unique business."

Because John Deere's workforce is aging due to contraction in the number of employees that resulted from hiring freezes during the difficult farming recession of the 1980s, most new hiring today is occurring at the college level in efforts of building a new generation of leaders. Mid-career hiring still occurs to meet changing needs, and these employees are given the same introduction to the John Deere way of conducting business as others.

One of the veterans responsible for developing the new generation of leaders is John Jenkins, the personable and hard-driving president of the Worldwide Commercial and Consumer Equipment division of John Deere. Jenkins leads a division that has a higher relative number of young and talented managers when compared to other divisions of the company because of the consumer nature of the product and the customer profile of those who buy the division's utility vehicles, all-terrain vehicles, and mowing equipment.

When Jenkins first left his position in corporate finance to lead an operating division, he became president of John Deere's Managed Health Care division. In his first operating position, he thought he would find volumes of compliance manuals on how to operate the business in line with corporate standards. There were none. Instead, management through the years focused on simple and clear messages of how to do business as opposed to compiling thousands of pages of documents.

Jenkins agrees with Mike Orr's assessment that the John Deere way is something you learn through osmosis, by adhering to a core set of values.

It's changing with the times, of course. As John Deere expands to even more locations around the globe, there may be a need to document work through guides and manuals that convey the proper ways of conducting business. However, there is still an emphasis on limiting the bureaucracy, and the tradition of John Deere employees learning from one another is ongoing.

ALL IN THE FAMILY

Not only are John Deere employees linked by time spent together at the company, but many also come from multigenerational John Deere families. This has occurred because in many of the communities where John Deere operates, jobs with the company are among the best to be found due to general stability, respect, and comfortable retirement offered.

Finding a John Deere employee whose father or mother worked at the company for 40 years is not uncommon. Neither is it uncommon to find employees whose grandfathers worked at the company. Others have brothers and sisters, cousins, and uncles working at John Deere. In these families, the John Deere lessons and lore have been passed down as a way of life, understood long before new generations earned their first company paycheck.

Jim Collins is one John Deere employee who has been with the company for 40 years and is still going strong. Today, Collins runs the John Deere Foundation from offices in downtown Moline. His father retired from Deere after 37 years and his brother worked at the company for 39 years. The John Deere way was as much a part of his heritage as genealogical roots. "With that kind of legacy," he said, "you almost have to do it the right way. You have to make sure you treat people right because it speaks not only for your employer, but also for your family."

This is also the case for Vicki Graves, senior vice president and legal counsel for John Deere Health Care. The 20-year John Deere employee's great-great-grandfather worked in John Deere's "wood department" in the days when wood was a major component for its plows and implements. Her great-grandfather painted tractors at John Deere for 50 years. Her grandmother worked as a John Deere secretary for a few years in the 1920s, and her father retired from John Deere as a parts information manager after almost 40 years on the job. As a fifth generation employee, Graves appreciates that her family, like so many others, has been able to benefit from working at a company that would never expect an employee to compromise values. "We've had two blue collars, one pink collar, and two white collars," she said. "Throughout the company and throughout the years, how we do business has been so defined and so recognized, it does not matter what division. It is practiced in health and insurance, just like it is practiced in all of the divisions at John Deere facilities throughout the world. "

THE BENEFITS OF BEING IN THE MIDDLE

Outside of the continuity in leadership and the workforce and the pass-along style of teaching and learning, the John Deere culture is rooted in a nonflashy, results-oriented approach to getting the job done. Shortcuts are frowned on and the prima donna is almost nonexistent, no matter the division or department. And due to the company's decentralized nature, the culture is one where employees solve problems at the source and take competitive pride within each separate division of the company. John Deere employees are almost always conservative in decision making, taking risks resulting from reasonable calculation.

John Deere may be global in vision and nature, but like the land from which it was born and where it still lies, John Deere is mainstream, generally in the middle when it comes to the style and daily approach to business.

"We don't always want to be the first or the last," said retired John Deere senior executive John Lawson. "That's kind of where Deere is positioned. We are not on the East Coast or the West Coast. We're in the middle. We started as an agricultural company and 95 percent of our products are still rooted in the ground and earth. That tends to emulate itself in the people. There are not a lot of flashy people at Deere and [the nonflashy] tend to perpetuate themselves. Yet the company remains a world leader by emphasizing not the superstar, but the accomplishments of many."

Some employees bristle at the thought that John Deere is defined by its rural, Midwestern presence. They are quick to point out that the company today is far more global than regional. After all, approximately 40 percent of the John Deere workforce is outside the United States. Still, few dispute that despite John Deere's strength and presence around the world, its culture has remained strong because one foot has remained firmly planted in the Midwestern soil.

The Quad Cities area is made up of four cities in two states along the Mississippi River, with many other smaller communities claiming to be part of the Quad Cities region. Moline, Illinois, is where Deere & Company has its world headquarters; Moline joins with Rock Island, Illinois, and Davenport and Bettendorf, Iowa, as the four core components of the Quad Cities. As late as the 1980s, the region was known as the farm implement capital of the world. Manufacturers of heavy equipment in the area at that time also included J.I. Case, International Harvester, and Caterpillar. All of those plants have now been closed; only Deere, now the leading employer in the region, remains. While not known as a cosmopolitan center, the Quad Cities are definitely based on Midwestern values and have an unassuming aura. The metropolitan area boasts almost 400,000 residents, but the cities maintain individual identities, creating at times a feeling of a smaller community. Almost everyone at John Deere, from entry-level employees to the company chairman, shops at the Wal-Mart.

The people worship at the same churches and their children usually go to the same schools. It's not that there's anything magic about the Midwest, but for John Deere, remaining located in a small, rural-at-heart metropolitan area, the value system of loyalty and hard work without pretension continues at the heart of the company culture.

"The value system is self-fulfilling," said Jim Jenkins, Deere's senior vice president and general counsel and an employee of just four years. "People self-select and bring these values in and they get reinforced. We've got to grow, and John Deere is always striving for new people and new ideas, but we never want to move away from our value system that begins with our heritage. Bob Lane has made that a top priority, constantly talking about *how* we do business. That's the one thing at John Deere that is nonnegotiable."

There were at least two times in John Deere's history, however, when heavy consideration was given to moving John Deere's headquarters from Moline. Under a plan discussed first during the leadership of Charles Deere Wiman in the 1950s and again in the 1990s during the leadership of Hans Becherer, John Deere would maintain central operations in Moline, but move executive offices to either San Francisco, New York, or Chicago, allowing more opportunity for top company officials to communicate with fellow business leaders and perhaps to broaden the recruitment pool available.

John Lawson remembers being on a committee considering the move the second time around. The concept got little support, he said, because even though there were some disadvantages with Moline, the advantages were far greater. Work is 10 minutes away. The airport is 10 minutes away. The golf course is 10 minutes away. The cost of living is less than in Chicago. Farms surround the community. Manufacturing plants are not far away. The environment represents the very customers that John Deere serves.

"[The culture] would be much more difficult to maintain if we were headquartered in a big city," said Sam Allen, who is president of Deere's financial services and power systems businesses as well as in charge of the company's worldwide human resources effort.

That statement is hard to argue against. For John Deere, being rooted in the Midwest has worked, because while the agriculture business as a whole has faced its economic ups and downs, two things besides product that have remained a constant at John Deere are the culture and commitment of its employees. If executives had been removed from the grounding spirit of the rural Midwest, it's likely that in the long-term, they would have become removed from the key differentiator for John Deere, a connection to the land and to the people who work it. And even though John Deere now has operations around the world, the fact that the global headquarters remains in Moline means that employees from all parts of the world must travel there on an ongoing basis for training and seminars, further reinforcing John Deere's commitment to its heritage.

ROOTED IN THE LAND

The unifying element of all the contributing factors of John Deere's thriving culture is the one that defines the many diverse products and services provided to customers: John Deere people, its products, and its mission are rooted in the land.

The company began serving farmers in 1837 and even though John Deere now operates multiple divisions, the agricultural division is still its largest. Other areas in products and services the company has expanded to over its history relate back to the lessons learned from experiences serving people who work the land, be it a farmer in California's Napa Valley or a housewife mowing her lawn in Connecticut.

This long-term tie to the land enables John Deere to maintain its focus when exploring growth, and it has provided a positive rub-off effect on employees and dealers who benefit from the of-the-soil spirit of customers, beginning with thousands of farmers from around the world. Former John Deere chairman and CEO Hans Becherer said global experiences taught him that most industries differ from country to country. Farming, however, is generally the same, whether it is in China, Sweden, Kenya, Canada, or the United States. People who work the soil anywhere share many values, and most have an affinity for John Deere because it stands for quality and longevity of doing business the right way.

"All farmers are salt of the earth kind of people,"

Becherer said. "The character of the company has been up-
lifted by the character of the customers. When a farmer gave
you a handshake, it meant you had a deal. People who work
the land share this integrity and loyalty."

He remembers serving a summer internship, while still
a graduate student, at the company's Harvester Works in
East Moline, which produces the company's highest-end
agricultural product, the combine. Becherer was trying to
decide whether to work for John Deere upon graduation. He
was talking one day after work to a John Deere janitor
sweeping the factory floor. The janitor noted it was raining
outside. "That's great," he said. "Rain helps the crops. That's
good for the farmer. And when the crops do well, we sell
more combines."

THE BENEFITS OF TEAMWORK

Whether they work on production lines in Waterloo or
Dubuque, or in executive offices in Moline, having employees
who understand the importance of pulling for the customer
and who understand there are few prima donnas among
46,000 people paid to work at John Deere is the ultimate benefit of the company's culture, according to Bob Lane.

He said John Deere is a company composed mostly of
ordinarily talented people, including himself. "We do have a
few geniuses, but most of us are not."

What John Deere does have, he remarked, for the most
part, is an unusual group of employees who are willing to

work together to make the company great. It is an undeniable secret to company success, Lane noted, that directly results from the strong John Deere culture that recognizes contributions of others at all levels.

"Our specialty," Lane said, "is getting people to work together. That's our leverage. Getting extraordinary results from ordinarily talented people is the essence of this company. When you get 46,000 people pulling together you can achieve remarkable results."

CHAPTER TWO

Quality Comes First

BUILT AT JOHN DEERE HARVESTER WORKS IN EAST MOLINE, the 9860 STS combine is not your average piece of heavy equipment. It is the largest and most productive agricultural machine ever built by John Deere and is guided in the field with precision by an AutoTrac steering system linked to a global positioning satellite. Able to unload up to 3.3 bushels of grain per second, the 375-horsepower combine is certainly the most coveted piece of agriculture equipment in the world.

Built at John Deere's Waterloo, Iowa, facility, a new 9020 John Deere tractor allows operators hands-free assisted steering through AutoTrac steering and features enhanced night vision for more productive after-dark work in the field. So efficient is the tractor that, if operated 24 hours a day with a 61-foot seeder attached, an operator can seed an astounding 3,800 acres in five days.

The big green machines redefine modern agricultural proficiency, but are major investments for farming operations of any size. A new 9860 STS combine costs almost $275,000. If new soybean and corn harvest headers are added, the price tag exceeds $300,000. A new 9020 tractor retails for almost $170,000. So when a customer places an order through a John Deere agricultural equipment dealership for a top-of-the-line tractor or combine, expectations are high that the product will live up to its reputation, not just at delivery, but after months and years of service.

For John Deere, the payoff to the customer is the promise of quality. The core value of building only quality products has been at the top the company's priority list since its founding in 1837. John Deere never wanted to send a plow out of his shop that was not built with the highest of standards, saying, "I will never put my name on a product that does not have in it the best that is in me." The conviction has remained with John Deere, becoming a major part of the culture and embraced at all levels.

All companies, of course, talk about quality at one time or another, but at John Deere it is not an initiative or a trend, particularly when product is involved. On assembly lines and in offices, employees have passed the value and its importance along to one another for generations. As a result, it is one area of business that is nonnegotiable, regardless of budget issues at hand or of whether the product is a John Deere Gator, a push lawn mower, or a high-end tractor. The promise of quality always comes first.

For the customer, quality begins with engineering and product design, continues at production facilities, and extends to dealerships. The quality promise at John Deere also now extends to all areas of the business, including finance, human resources, and supplier relationships. It does not mean that every single finished product coming off assembly

---

The John Deere Quality Initiative

- Selling and supporting products and services that consistently meet high expectations of customers for performance, reliability, durability, and maintainability.
- Establishing a work environment in which dedicated employees can achieve their personal and professional objectives while making the company successful.
- Achieving consistent and predictable financial results that meet investor expectations.
- Maintaining relationships that lead to success for all.

---

lines is built perfectly, nor does it mean that mistakes are never made in other areas of the business. But Bob Lane said that by demonstrating an "unwavering insistence on quality" and aiming only for the highest standards, John Deere can deliver the value that customers, employees, shareholders, and other business partners expect, every time they interact with the company.

THE GOLD KEY

At the customer level, one way John Deere conveys its commitment to quality in its higher-end products is through a program that allows buyers to see their actual purchase on the assembly line and meet some of the workers who assembled it. With Gold Key, buyers of John Deere combines and large tractors may receive an invitation to visit manufacturing facilities in either East Moline, Illinois, or Waterloo, Iowa. As well, construction equipment customers are invited to experience similar welcomes at factories that build their equipment.

Typically arranged with the customer by the John Deere dealer, plans are made after the combines or large tractors are ordered for a trip to the factory that coincides with the estimated completion date of the product on the assembly line. The buyer, often joined by friends and family, is given a tour of the plant. Near the end of the line, buyers are introduced to their actual product, given a working gold key, and invited to climb into the cab. Workers often gather around as the buyer becomes the first one to start the ignition among cheers and best wishes.

The program and atmosphere uniquely links customers, product, and the people who build the product with its on-site interaction. The dealer gets the benefit of rewarding buyers and allowing them a behind-the-scenes look at their purchase. Production workers get to see smiles on faces of customers, who appreciate their attention to detail and interest in getting it right. Customers get first-hand reinforcement of the John Deere quality promise, not to mention a close-up look at some of the world's more unique manufacturing facilities.

First opened in 1913 to manufacture horse-drawn harvesting equipment, John Deere Harvester Works in East Moline is a sprawling facility that covers almost 200 acres. Tours are given by retired employees who shuttle guests on motorized carts past stamping and assembly. Production workers often nod and wave, and visitors on the 90-minute tour see displays made by workers ranging from antique equipment to pledges of quality. A highlight is usually the site of the giant combine bodies receiving their final touches of John Deere green paint by mechanical arms, but the best is always the last.

Ron Wilson of Decker, Indiana, knows firsthand. His family had used John Deere equipment on its 90-year-old farm for years, but his first factory visit came after purchasing a new 60 Series combine. Although Lou Gehrig's disease required him to use a wheelchair, Wilson said John Deere employees went out of their way to get him into the cab of the combine to make sure he was the very first to turn the key.

John Deere's Waterloo Works, where tractor buyers take the Gold Key tour, is the company's largest manufacturing facility, consisting of five sites totaling more than 13 million square feet. Undergoing a $125 million upgrade designed to improve production cycle times by 75 percent, reduce inventory by 25 percent, remove two million square feet of floor space, and facilitate build-to-demand, the plant is to tractor manufacturing in the early twenty-first century what Ford Motor Company's Rouge complex was to auto manufacturing in the early twentieth century.

No plant in the world builds tractors like Waterloo, a part of John Deere since 1918, as customers like Roman Stoltzfoos of Gap, Pennsylvania, know. He bought his new John Deere 7210 tractor from the Deer Creek Equipment dealership, which has three locations, and took a trip to Waterloo with his sons Dwight and Delmar to watch it come off the line. Each took a turn in the cab, starting the tractor with the Gold Key as production workers watched the family's experience with their newest investment.

BACKING UP THE PROMISE

Quality, however, is more than executing a well-built product on the assembly line at John Deere, because even though the company strives for and is known for its product quality, no manufacturing company is perfect and problems can occasionally occur.

"Are we known for quality because we always get it right the first time?" Lane said. "Sadly, we're not, because often enough, it has not worked out that way. But if we don't get it right the first time, people know we will stand behind it. That's what we do at John Deere. Customers know this from years of experience."

Dating back to the days of John Deere's two-cylinder tractors, the company developed a reputation and ethic for supporting its equipment through its dealership network that continues today. Whether a customer buys a tractor from a dealer in Arkansas or a riding lawn mower from a Home Depot store in California, there is a John Deere dealer nearby who provides full service on the product. It is how the company extends its promise beyond the factory, while for the customer, it is the ultimate assurance of quality, knowing that problems can always be solved without having to take drastic measures to transport or ship products to faraway locations for service and repair.

"Fixing mistakes," Lane said, "is an expensive way to do business. It costs us in reputation, not just on the bottom line. We must continuously seek improvement in our quality."

It is John Deere's commitment to the customer and the heart of its brand promise of quality. But Lane and John Deere are pushing to eliminate mistakes on the front end, hoping the emphasis will contribute substantially to the goal of becoming a great business.

John Deere's most significant means of improving initial product quality today is through its lean, flexible, and disciplined manufacturing style that is being adopted at worldwide plants. Many times in manufacturing, poor quality results from the overburdened factory. Improvements in productivity yield quality improvements as well, which is one reason the company initiated the John Deere Production System in 2001, and it has been adopted by many of the company's 50 manufacturing sites since.

The system was necessary because with so many factories and with multiple divisions building entirely different equipment, John Deere had processes that were all over the board in terms of technique and approach. By developing one manufacturing process, employing it and improving it, the company can better manage production and quality on a large scale.

Much like the trend in automotive manufacturing, John Deere's system is based on flexibility, allowing multiple products to be built in different cycles at the same location. Plants are more responsive to actual current demand, reducing inventory and increasing production times.

Basic Principles of the John Deere Production System

- **An engaged and flexible workforce**—Addresses structured processes to support specific tasks and to encourage workforce flexibility and openness to change.
- **Enabling manufacturing technology and processes**—Focuses on new technology that supports innovation, maximum performance, and speed.
- **Integrated production and material logistics planning**—Presents methods for synchronizing production with customer demand to support order fulfillment strategies such as sales and operations planning. Key ingredients include replenishing inventory on demand and establishing a pull system.
- **Reliable and repeatable processes and equipment**—Incorporates approaches for building quality into products the first time, continuously improving that quality, and then maintaining the improvements.
- **Leadership**—Provides vision, expectations, and recognition for success that guides the necessary cultural changes.

BEYOND MANUFACTURING

At John Deere, however, nuts and bolts assembly is only one small part of the continual quest for quality. Employees in all divisions of the company have learned through years of experience that quality is a core issue in every aspect of the business, ranging from finance to human resources to purchasing.

Pierre Leroy is president of John Deere's Construction and Forestry Equipment division. Born in Haiti, Leroy was raised in Chicago after his physician parents had to flee their home country because his father was sought by a government official after refusing to sign a false death certificate. After receiving an undergraduate degree from the University of Michigan and an MBA from the University of Chicago, Leroy went to work for Goldman Sachs, where his career took off. When an opportunity came to interview with John Deere, he was reluctant but ultimately was swayed by the quality of the people he met, giving up a higher salary to come to work at Deere.

In the Finance department Leroy was given a difficult assignment, to determine if John Deere could afford to remain in the finance business. The company had suffered during economic upturns because the Credit division ate cash. He visited banks and came up with a plan, eventually doing a deal for John Deere that was an original for its time, asset-backed securities. As a result, Credit was financed with very little capital and became one of John Deere's most reliably profitable divisions.

Leroy quickly rose through the ranks of the company, serving as CFO before taking over the Construction and Forestry Equipment division. There, his challenge is seemingly as great as solving the dilemma for the Credit division years ago, because in construction equipment, Caterpillar is the world leader, enjoying a position as strong in that industry as John Deere commands in agriculture.

Deere's construction equipment business has made great gains from its start 45 years ago when it was essentially begun to fill a small-equipment niche overlooked by Caterpillar and others that were manufacturing construction equipment. With more experience and the desire to grow, John Deere began to build bigger products and slowly increase its presence in the industry. Today, John Deere competes with Caterpillar in several key product categories with a divisionwide commitment to quality and customer service.

But quality extends far beyond John Deere production lines and dealerships. A total quality effort in the construction equipment division has created an atmosphere in which employees understand that quality in their daily work ultimately results in the quality that customers see and feel when they get behind the wheel of a new, yellow Deere 710 backhoe loader.

When the construction and forestry equipment division fostered a culture of total business quality, employees for the first time began to see how quality impacts the cost structure in every area of the business. And, by analyzing each component one by one, the processes are customized, delivering lasting results.

In 2003 the quality team's focus was sales and marketing.

Working with a multidisciplinary group from within the company, John Deere's Construction and Forestry Equipment quality team developed the Signature Process for dealers, designed to be an end-to-end program from customers to dealers to the company.

As the division quality initiative neared completion in 2004, Leroy said he was seeing dramatic results. "The change," he said, "in terms of dollars and cents is easy. To create real change, you need to change the way people feel and think about the work. When that happens, the pride becomes evident."

In the end, the pride is what keeps John Deere employees in all divisions constantly striving to attain the highest level of quality in every aspect of the business.

CHAPTER THREE

Create Change
through Innovation

JOHN DEERE DOES NOT OPERATE ON THE BLEEDING EDGE OF technology and design because of its quest to deliver quality and durability, but the company has maintained a creative mindset throughout its history that has separated it from competitors over time. As a result, some of what Bob Lane calls the most important "hinge years" in the company's history are colored by visionary stretch and new standards when it comes to innovation and looking toward the future.

The company, of course, won't sacrifice its core promise of quality to customers just for the sake of sending out a press release about flashy new product dynamics. But John Deere has shown throughout its history an ability to strategically raise the bar of innovation and creativity at the right moments and in the right places. Each time, it has made all the difference.

It's a mindset inside the company that dates back to founder John Deere. His self-scouring plow changed the agricultural business for many farmers in the Midwest who learned of its distinct advantage. But even though John Deere sold 2,000 plows in 1849 and was on its way to

---

John Deere's Commitment to Innovation

Innovation means inventing, designing and developing breakthrough products and services that customers want to buy from John Deere. Strategic investment in research and development is a mainstay of the company as we constantly strive to delight customers with products and services that help them realize their own aspirations of effectiveness and efficiency.

---

large-scale commercial success, he was continually working through field tests and discussions with farmers to gain information that could be used to improve his product. If a farmer suggested improvements, they were made. Or, if Deere himself discovered a change or alteration that would improve the plow, the change was made. He was constantly copying, reflecting, and experimenting in a quest for improvement.

Robert Tate, a former business partner of Deere's, recalled in his diary a disagreement with the company founder that lives on today in company lore. "Farmers have to buy what we make," said Tate, apparently tiring of Deere's never-ending quest for plow improvement.

"Damn the odds," Deere responded. "They don't have to buy what we make. We have to continually improve our trade or we're going to lose it."

The company enhanced and expanded its product lines rapidly through the 1870s, manufacturing full lines of plows, cultivators, harrows, drills, and planters, wagons and buggies, and in 1875 took farmers off their feet when plowing fields with production of the Gilpin Silky Plow.

A PIVOTAL ACQUISITION

When John Deere embarked on one of the most important changes in its history, the company founder who had invented the plow was no longer alive. Nor was his son, Charles Deere. But in drawing from the early lessons set by the founder and his commitment to constantly improving his trade, CEO William Butterworth (husband of Charles Deere's daughter, Katherine) overcame initial reluctance and led the company to make in 1918 an acquisition that set the manufacturer on a new course that continues to define John Deere today.

Most farm machinery dependent upon the horse had been discovered by 1891, and although John Deere was a leading manufacturer of plows and implements in America after the turn of the century—sales in 1916 were $28.1 million and company employees numbered almost 7,000—competitors were entering the growing tractor business as it became apparent to all with the emergence of the automobile that horses would give way, even in the fields. Deere & Company developed its own prototype tractors beginning in 1914 when board member Joseph Dain was asked to study the situation of the fast-emerging gas-powered machinery.

There was concern at John Deere, though, as to whether the company could compete with manufacturers like Ford Motor Company, which was entering the market with its own gas tractor. Butterworth himself stated bluntly in 1916 that he wanted John Deere to stop its costly effort of trying to develop a prototype tractor worth manufacturing, believing sales would be low due to competition which had a head start and more experience with engine works. He wanted the company to focus its efforts on its successful plow business, providing implements for leading manufacturers.

Ultimately, though, it was decided at John Deere that the tractor was coming, and if the company was to be a leading manufacturer in agricultural equipment, it would have to be involved with the tractor in some way. John Deere employee W.R. Morgan, manager of the Harvester Works in 1918, heard that the tractor plant of Waterloo Boy in Waterloo, Iowa, might be for sale. Founded in 1895, Waterloo Boy had produced a popular and respected two-cylinder kerosene tractor since 1911. In 1917 the company had produced more than 4,000 tractors, which weighed more than 5,000 pounds and sold for around $1,000.

After moving its headquarters to Moline, Illinois, in 1848, John Deere had prospered for more than 60 years as leading manufacturer of horse drawn plows and had an efficient system of selling products through its "branch houses," or marketing centers. But overnight and with little fanfare, the company became one of the nation's top producers of the gas-powered, two-cylinder tractor when the board of directors agreed in 1918 to pay $2,350,000 to purchase the Waterloo Gasoline Traction Engine Company. In John Deere's first year in the tractor business, the company sold 5,634 Waterloo Boy machines.

"The technology had yet to be proven, and it wasn't even clear at the time that the tractor had what it took to replace the horse," Lane said. "Still, the risk was considered worthwhile because it had the potential to accomplish great good—for the farmers who would be the consumers of the product, the craftsmen who would earn their living manufacturing it, and for the investors who wanted an honest profit on the capital they had invested in the corporation."

By 1937, less than 20 years after the Waterloo tractor acquisition, John Deere reached the $100 million plateau in gross sales and the company, under the leadership of John Deere's great-grandson, Charles Deere Wiman, had strengthened its post-depression position as a top manufacturer with the introduction of its A and B models. The tractors were popular, but like competitive products of the time, the design was essentially utilitarian. Most people then viewed agricultural equipment as tools to be based purely on raw functionality, with little consideration for operator comfort and appeal. John Deere engineers had a different idea, however. They wanted to contact Henry Dreyfuss, a man who had emerged as a pioneer in industrial design. Seeking to distance the John Deere brand from competition, Henry Dreyfuss and Associates of New York was commissioned by Deere & Company in 1938 to work with company engineers in streamlining the A and B series tractors. The goal was to blend John Deere's trademark functionality with attractive design.

It was an unparalleled move in the agricultural machine industry at the time, the concept of a leading manufacturer contacting a New York designer to consult about the look and feel of a tractor. Only one company, Oliver Hart-Parr, had introduced styled tractors and it was not a major competitor of Deere & Company like International Harvester. For the most part, tractors were still regarded only for utility as the distance between the Big Apple and rural farms in the Midwest in the 1930s was far greater than it appeared to be on the map. Style was generally reserved for the big cities, since electricity and running water were still luxuries for many on the farm, and design was not an obvious concern with most.

THE MAN IN THE BROWN SUIT

Born in New York in 1904 and educated in the arts, Henry Dreyfuss was "in essence, a plain and simple man" who always "wore a brown suit, no matter the occasion," according to John Deere archivist Neil Dahlstrom. Dreyfuss had worked as a young man in theatre before opening his own industrial design office in New York in 1927. He had a natural understanding for making bulky and awkward industrial objects sleek and more user-friendly. Whether it was color, shape, size, or the addition or subtraction of parts, he loved to make the complex simple through refinement. His business had started slowly, but by the early 1930s he started to obtain more corporate clients and designed such items as hinges, keys, toasters, kitchen utensils, and a thermostat for Honeywell that incorporated a clock into its display.

When Deere & Company called on his services, it was through an unannounced visit to his New York office by one of the engineers from the Waterloo Tractor facility, Elmer McCormick, who had taken a train to meet the acclaimed designer and wore a fur coat and a straw hat on arrival. McCormick's enthusiasm persuaded Dreyfuss to join him on the return train home to Waterloo the next day to meet with John Deere engineers.

John Deere tractors had shown character beginning with the Model D (1923), the first one to bear the John Deere name, and the company's traditional green and yellow scheme had identified John Deere tractors to customers since 1924. But new styling resulted from planning with Dreyfuss that redesigned the Model A and B tractors into more streamlined looks and included such features as rubber tires, electric starting, and lights as options.

Company advertising showed "Sister" and "Bud" taking turns at the wheel, signifying the product's appeal beyond its utility advantages. The Model B would become John Deere's bestselling tractor for more than 15 years and many inside the company learned in the process that a little style and innovative functionality blended with reliability and utility go a long way with customers.

DEERE DAY IN DALLAS

Before 1960, all John Deere tractors were powered by two cylinders and the engine was mounted horizontally, allowing operators to easily service them as their own mechanics. The argument was made by engineers at John Deere to move away from the two-cylinder tractor—known as Poppin' Johnnies due to the sound made by the exhaust—because of the engine system's limited power. John Deere engineers had devised ingenious ways to juice up power of the two-cylinder through such means as using a fuel mixture and intake through separate carburetors. As modern, rural America advanced and demands on the farm increased, the need for more powerful tractors became a bigger issue.

In 1955, John Deere chairman Charles Deere Wiman and Bill Hewitt, his successor, who was company president at the time, wanted to radically redesign John Deere tractors, adding power and style simultaneously. They launched a major product development program with the intent of abandoning the trademark two-cylinder engine. This meant John Deere had to find ways of fitting a new, larger engine in tractors esthetically, increasing the need for an all-new product design. The tractor program was risky—almost all tractors and farm equipment were made the same in America in the mid-1950s because time and money were so precious that farmers were generally not willing to heavily invest in untried and unproven equipment.

Also, most farm equipment manufacturers were not accustomed to spending excessive dollars on risky product development for the simple fact that what they had already worked. Farmers were buying the existing products, and it was easier to just keep taking more profits from them. But John Deere pushed ahead with the new tractor program anyway, convinced the company could gain distance from its closest competitors. The company's new generation of power sparked a farming revolution in the fields of America.

The design expertise of Henry Dreyfuss was once again utilized (John Deere's relationship with Henry Dreyfuss and Associates continued after the designer's death in 1972 and still exists today). Dreyfuss debated the tractor's color for some time, but decided to leave it green. As for the larger, more powerful engine, he managed to conceal it underneath a shaped, one-piece metal hood which "contributed to the visual impression that the vehicle was in the process of pulling, reinforcing the added power."

Dreyfuss also demanded that visible seams, screws, or anything that detracted from an impression of massiveness be avoided, allowing the tractor to appear sleek and refined. Seats were designed with heavy input from Dreyfuss as he sought to remove the typical holes that served as ventilation on the steel seat with smaller, more comfortable slits. This modification resulted in a moving, three-piece seat on a metal support that allowed the operator to adjust it according to size, using a quick-release lever.

Even like the earth itself, and that special breed of men who till and seed and nurture it and reap its bounty, the implements of agriculture have a frugal, rugged, no-nonsense quality even amid today's mechanical sophistication. The engineers at Deere understand this and want their multitude of farm machines to reflect Deere's long experience: utility, simplicity, durability, safety and—for men who live long hours in wind and sun—comfort. For this client, we integrate the design of products made at many plants to do many kinds of work in America and overseas. By fitting machine to Man, we perpetuate a product "look" that echoes a company's creed and tradition.

—Henry Dreyfuss (1904–1972)

In a masterful marketing move led by CEO Bill Hewitt, John Deere's New Generation of Power tractors were unveiled at a large-scale, company-sponsored event called Deere Day in Dallas in 1960. Like the new tractors—John Deere first released two new four-cylinder models from Dubuque and two new six-cylinder models from Waterloo—Dallas was in 1960 a blend of rural toughness and urban sophistication, making it the perfect backdrop for unveiling the new products to the world. For visual impact, John Deere shipped 136 new tractors and 324 other pieces of other machinery in secrecy to a parking lot near Dallas' Cotton Bowl stadium. Thousands of John Deere dealers, journalists, and guests from around the country were invited and flown in to Dallas to see John Deere's new tractors. Most would get to see, touch, and feel the products in the parking lot near the Cotton Bowl, but not until after a stylish unveiling that, becoming of the new design, was held in, of all places, the Neiman Marcus department store.

The tractor was positioned inside the store near the jewelry counter, but it was hidden from curious onlookers inside a large gift box, wrapped in a bow, and adorned with a card telling shoppers they "would soon see something they had never seen before." Standing in front of the box for the August 30, 1960, unveiling were Hewitt, his wife Tish, Henry Dreyfuss, and Stanley Marcus. Standing beside the box was a model in sequined overalls. Cameras flashed as Tish Hewitt took shears from a velvet cushion and cut the bow, revealing a styled, more powerful four-cylinder tractor bearing the John Deere name. It was decorated with diamonds and its green and yellow paint glistened on the Neiman Marcus floor. And for perhaps the first time in American history, the farm was fashionable and hip.

So moved was Hewitt that he boldly predicted the new tractors would lead John Deere to overcome competitor International Harvester as the world's leading provider of farm and industrial tractors and equipment. His prediction came true, since less than four years later, John Deere sales had increased by almost 60 percent (from $510 million in sales in 1960 to $816 million in sales in 1964) and the company had added more than 11,000 new employees. John Deere did pass International Harvester in 1963 to become the world's largest producer and seller of farm and industrial tractors and equipment, a position it has never relinquished. In the same year, the company ventured into the consumer market, deciding to produce and sell lawn and garden tractors as well as mowers and snow blowers.

"[Hewitt] laid down the gauntlet," said Bob Lane, "and inaugurated a permanent degree of success for this company."

A BUILDING TO REFLECT THE MISSION

It has been said that to properly identify the personality of a company, one should only stand outside its headquarters for a few moments and gaze. That's certainly the case with John Deere. The building known as the Deere & Company World Headquarters rests timelessly and transparently against a flowing landscape of water, trees, manicured lawn, and rural tranquillity. Like the company, the building is rooted in the land by design and rises effortlessly from the ground like the trees it blends among. John Deere's 1,400-acre headquarters site is just seven miles from downtown Moline. It was chosen by John Deere in the mid-1950s as the site for the company's new administration center when its facilities by the Mississippi River began showing age. Remembered for his sense of humor, appreciation of history, and competitive fire, Bill Hewitt is best known at John Deere for his appreciation of style and willingness to pursue it for the company for long-term gain at short-term expense. Nothing signifies his vision better than the company's headquarters facility in Moline.

Just as Hewitt pushed John Deere to begin its new tractor program while president of the company in 1955, he began pushing a plan as chairman less than two years later to
build a new, state-of-the-art administration center. Deere's
facilities in downtown Moline in the 1950s were typical of
the area and period, conservative Midwest offices that ran
together between warehouses built for necessity of expansion rather than for aesthetic quality.

Hewitt, however, saw the company as a more global,
planned, and timeless entity than one that was regional
and planned haphazardly. John Deere was expanding into
developing agricultural regions outside the United States
like Mexico, and Hewitt believed John Deere needed a
headquarters facility to reflect its global presence and quest
for excellence on company employees. So when Hewitt
went looking for an architect to fulfill this mission, he
contracted with one of the best in the world at the time,
Eero Saarinen.

Noted for designing American facilities such as Dulles
International Airport in Washington, D.C., and the General
Motors Technical Center in Warren, Michigan, Finnish-
born Saarinen was seen by some members of the company's
board as a stretch both in dollars and taste, considering that
John Deere had for 120 years occupied facilities far more
humble than he was likely to propose. But Hewitt was con-
vincing in his views that a world-class facility would better
represent contemporary John Deere. The company engaged
Saarinen for architecture just as it had engaged Dreyfuss for

product design years before. When writing to Saarinen on August 23, 1957, Hewitt said,

> The men who created this company and caused it to grow and flourish were men of strength—rugged, honest, close to the soil. Since the company's early days, quality of product and integrity in relationships with farmers, dealers, suppliers and the public in general have been Deere's guiding factors.
>
> In thinking of our traditions and our future, and in thinking of the people who will work in or visit our new headquarters, I believe it should be thoroughly modern in concept, but at the same time down to earth and rugged.

Hewitt got his wish. Although Saarinen died just after the contract for construction was signed in 1961, he had designed a facility for John Deere that is as contemporary and useful today as it was upon completion in 1964. Taking advantage of the site that consisted of high and low river land with wooded ravines, Saarinen used strong, dark buildings positioned above a manmade lake to give occupants the feeling of being up in the trees. John Deere's world headquarters is a seven-story silhouette of glass and unfinished steel, providing an open, outside view from every office.

At a construction cost of $8 million, the building allowed flexible future expansion (walls and interior structures are interchangeable, making reconfiguration easy) and uniquely represents the character of John Deere. "No brashly modern or pretentious building would have been right," Saarinen said. "Farm machinery is not slick, shiny or metal, but forged from iron and steel in big, forceful, functional shapes."

He used exposed steel and used a unique system of sunshading with metal louvers which cut out sun 90 percent of the time and eliminate the need for curtains and blinds. The design was a complex of three buildings, initially intended to house about 900 employees. The main office building, which is seven stories high, rises from the floor of a wooded ravine and faces two ponds. A glass-enclosed bridge connects the main building to a product-display building and a 400-seat auditorium. The building looks nothing like its age today, with hallways decorated with one of the world's best corporate art collections and major architectural awards from as recently as the 1990s.

THE IMPORTANCE OF PRODUCT REINVESTMENT

John Deere's quest for innovation in products and design has continued throughout the company's history, even in years money was so tight during farm recessions that spending heavily on future products seemed foolish to some. John Lawson was with the company for 44 years and never remembers a time anyone suggested cutting back on research and development spending, even in the toughest times.

Even during the severe contraction in the agricultural industry in the 1980s, John Deere did more, in fact, injecting more torque, more power, and more functionality into its tractors and combines. During the toughest times, the main objective from the company's earliest days has never wavered, to serve customers through innovation regardless of the times.

That's why the company invested heavily in new product again in 2001, despite difficult conditions in agriculture and the greater economy. Some agricultural manufacturers were delaying the development of new products. John Deere launched more than 50 new products designed specifically for the agricultural market. The most notable were the new 8020 and 8020T Series tractors, which redefined power control. Profits were dropping as conditions worsened, yet John Deere took "aggressive actions to further strengthen our competitiveness."

"The eighties were particularly tough," Lawson said. "We would go to product review meetings and the chairman and all the top executives were there to participate. We needed to cut costs, but engineering was always supported. And I don't remember a time when Deere delayed the next generation of product.

"There was an understanding that we had an obligation to deliver."

Today, Lawson likes to reflect over the John Deere product line as it evolved during the 40-plus years he worked at the company. He takes a walk at the John Deere Pavilion where products are on display and is amazed at the changes in size, strength, and design that have occurred since the company moved from two-cylinder tractors in 1960.

The changes through the years have not occurred just in existing John Deere products like plows, but in recent developments as well, many of which still include influences from the late Henry Dreyfuss. The company's experience with the industrial designer was profound, extending beyond tractors and even the man himself. In addition to his product design contributions, Dreyfuss influenced everything from the redesign of the company trademark and graphics to corporate films and often assisted in the selection of oil paintings, tapestries, and sculpture for the world headquarters. He also encouraged Hewitt to hire Eero Saarinen to design the headquarters facility. When Dreyfuss died in 1972, John Deere continued working closely on projects with his company, Henry Dreyfuss and Associates.

BLAZING NEW GROUND

Few products exemplify this concept better than the popular John Deere Gator, the off-road utility vehicle that continues to find new markets because of its multiple uses. Just as Apple's iPod is creating a new segment in personal music-listening devices, John Deere's Gator launched a new market for off-road utility vehicles. Co-developed by John Deere engineers and Henry Dreyfuss and Associates, the product was an award winner and apparently a much-needed alternative to all-terrain vehicles (ATVs).

Developed in the 1980s and first manufactured at John Deere's Welland (Ont.) factory in 1987, the Gator utility vehicle is a unique blend of power and rugged flamboyance that appealed first to the military and pro football teams as effective means of transporting equipment and the injured. The Gator travels up to 20 miles an hour (unless retrofitted or for a specific use) and features a steering wheel and pedals for easier operation than traditional ATVs, which use motorcycle-like controls. It ferries passengers more comfortably than a traditional golf cart and has the power to climb rugged hills and transport heavy cargo.

Special editions have been adapted for the military, and when special equipment was needed to traverse the piles of rubble at Ground Zero after the September 11, 2001, attacks, John Deere sent in 50 Gators to Staten Island, which were then ferried to Ground Zero, where rescue workers put them to work. Sales of the popular Gator have grown significantly since production began, and variations and uses continue to multiply.

In the beginning, though, some John Deere dealers and customers did not know what they had in the Gator, and machines sat idle on lots. Said Richard Miller, whose dealership is near Nashville: "I sold them mainly as toys for big boys." But Miller recalls that when customers "began to realize how versatile this piece of equipment is," sales took off.

Thrilled with the Gator's success, John Deere expanded

the line, creating such variations as a TurfGator for golf courses—its tires don't scar greens—and making available such implements as stretcher beds for sports teams and the military. The result is a product line that is popular with a broad base of users ranging from small landowners to sports team physicians to golf course superintendents and contractors, who find many uses for the off-road utility sporting the John Deere green.

MORE TO COME

John Deere's spending in research and development is a reason the company has maintained an innovative edge throughout its history. John Deere spends more than its major competitors on research and development as a percentage of net sales, searching for tomorrow's solutions. In 2003, for example, the John Deere Agricultural Equipment division invested 4 percent of its net sales in research and development, almost two times what its largest competitors spent. Additionally, competitors such as AGCO spread dollars across multiple brands, while John Deere supports just one with its dollars. This focus on innovation allows John Deere to be a leader, helping its customers find more productivity.

In 1837, this meant manufacturing a plow that kept sticky soil from clinging to its sides. In 1960, this meant building a tractor that combined more power, comfort, and style than farmers had seen before. In 2005, this means producing a combine that uses such advanced technology as global satellite positioning to guide the equipment on the most productive path, while enabling farmers to better control input costs and yields through its state-of-the-art systems.

Bob Lane believes John Deere can do more, not necessarily in terms of spending, but in creativity and vision in line with the company's core value of innovation. "There's a limit to how much bigger and stronger a combine can get," he said, "but they can be smarter. If we reduce the time a farmer spends driving in the field and increase the information about the crop available to the farmer in the cab, he can put more of his effort into increasing his profitability."

Lane said John Deere is at times "innovation slow, invention light and customer focus hazy." He notes that while the company owns some patents, it often employs technologies developed by others to build its products. In agriculture, for instance, this mission to be the innovation leader may not mean developing something as radical as an all-new tractor, but instead finding technology that helps the farmer improve efficiency through more accurate seeding methods. In construction, it means designing equipment that changes the way contractors prepare sites to dramatically improve efficiency.

One example: The John Deere 1690 Soybean Special ($73,000 retail), a planter, accurately meters seed to each row, ensuring even spacing, maximum plant growth, and even yield for farmers. Another example: the Military R-Gator, built through a partnership of John Deere and iRobot, with full production slated to begin by 2006, an intelligent unmanned ground vehicle that will use off-the-shelf technology to autonomously perform dangerous and taxing missions.

John Deere has a long history of developing products that improve its customers' productivity, and Lane's commitment to do more, faster in the future underscores the company's commitment to use innovation as a driving force of creating change.

CHAPTER FOUR

Always Maintain Integrity

OF JOHN DEERE'S FOUR CORE VALUES, THE ONE THAT MAY BE most responsible for the company's endurance is the on-going resolution by employees to conduct business with integrity, no matter what. Most companies strive for innovation and talk about quality, but few have placed integrity at the top of the importance pyramid and have never replaced it for a moment. For John Deere, however, integrity is a distinguishing characteristic that will not be compromised.

Company founder John Deere, although prone to becoming overextended, laid the foundation of doing business the right way, conducting himself in the office and in the community with zest, honesty, and a do-unto-others approach with all people. Known for spending generous amounts of money and time in community churches and charitable organizations, John Deere believed all people should have opportunity and that fairness was a social equalizer.

This characteristic was passed on to his son Charles Deere, who began working at the company at age 16 and learned from his father. "I will never," said Charles Deere, "from this seventh day of February, Eighteen Hundred and Sixty A.D., put my name to a paper that I do not expect to pay—so help me God." He ran the company for 49 years, almost twice as long as his father, so by the time he died in 1907 and son-in-law William Butterworth took over as chief executive officer, the importance of integrity as a core value within the company was firmly established.

Several times during John Deere's history, integrity has led to defining and shifting moments. The first was during the Great Depression in the early 1930s, when difficult financial decisions were made to support employees and customers. A major embezzlement occurred in 1931 at the bank that held the savings of most employees that threatened the financial security of thousands of them. People's Savings Bank in Moline was closely linked to Deere & Company because one of its founders was Charles Deere

---

John Deere's Commitment to Integrity

Integrity means telling the truth, keeping our word and treating others with fairness and respect. It is demonstrated through honest relationships, effective decisions that consider the balanced interests of all those who have an interest in our success, and unquestioned commitment to ethical and legal behavior. We intend to live by these expectations for the long term. Our reputation is based in large part on our desire to always act with integrity and this is one of our most valued assets.

and its president in 1931 was William Butterworth. Thousands of John Deere employees patronized the bank, which had been in existence for 74 years, and the company maintained a checking account with more than $2 million.

State bank examiners determined that a cashier and two others inside People's Savings Bank had embezzled more than $1.2 million over time and had wasted most of the money on poor real estate investments—meaning the loss was in large part not recoverable. William Butterworth was chairman of John Deere at the time in Washington, D.C. serving a second term as president of the U.S. Chamber of Commerce. Company president Charles Deere Wiman was faced with a difficult decision when notified of the embezzlement: Pay the bank's loss or allow the state bank examiner to foreclose, threatening the savings of so many Deere & Company employees during the increasingly difficult Depression.

"As I view it," Wiman told fellow Deere & Company board members on the day a decision had to be made, "there are approximately seven million of savings deposits in this bank, largely made by the wage earners of our factories, and the effects upon them of the closing of the bank, and the resulting consequences to this company, are beyond calculation."

The next day, Deere & Company wrote a check to the People's Savings Bank of Moline in the amount of $1.29 million. When word of the embezzlement spread around town, it was with the assurance that the company had covered the loss, and patrons did not make a run on the bank, depleting it of deposits. The bank remained open for two more years before a new bank was formed in 1933—the Moline National Bank—to pick up the pieces of People's Savings Bank, which was dissolved. Deere & Company owned 90 percent of the stock for Moline National Bank and made sure over time that depositors transferred in the action suffered no losses due to continuing problems at People's Savings Bank.

A HELPING HAND

As the Depression hardened from 1930 to 1933, the financial situation for many John Deere employees and customers worsened. Company sales plunged from $64 million in 1930 to just $8.7 million in 1933, forcing massive layoffs, pay and pension cuts, and an end to paid vacations and shortened hours for remaining employees. In all, 70 percent of the workforce was laid off over a three-year span, but John Deere responded by continuing group health insurance for those out of a job and lowering rent in company housing.

Farmers were faring no better during the Depression as severe drought in the Great Plains combined with the severe financial stress to put many farmers at least temporarily out of business. John Deere carried millions of dollars in receivables from farmers owing debts on financed equipment, and most could not afford to make payments due to the severity of the Depression and drought. John Deere had two choices:

Collect through repossession or lend a compassionate hand by carrying the debts with hopes of collecting later when farm conditions improved. They chose the latter, carrying debtor farmers through the period with no penalties. Many John Deere customers are still loyal to the company because their families were able to keep their land and farms during the Depression because of the company.

The Depression was particularly painful for the company, though, as it suffered heavy financial losses ($4 million in 1932) and significant internal stress due to the hardship of so many. No one took it harder than Wiman, who absorbed most of the decision-making responsibility in the absence of Butterworth. But something Wiman and John Deere did in addition to providing relief for employees and customers was continuing product development at an aggressive pace. Despite the fact that sales of new John Deere equipment were reduced to almost nothing in 1932 and 1933, Wiman pushed the company to develop new products, resulting in the Model A and the Model B tractors, which would ultimately become best-selling products.

Ultimately, as difficult as the Depression was for John Deere, history shows that the company's commitment to product and loyalty to its employees and core customers was a major turning point in its history. The company emerged from the Depression with advantages over competition due to stronger customer loyalty and new products. By 1936, John Deere was closing in on the significant market leadership position enjoyed by its largest rival, International Harvester.

CLEAR COMMUNICATION OF
ABIDING PRINCIPLES

For many years, stories that enforced John Deere philosophies and core values passed from employee to employee and generation to generation verbally, on manufacturing floors, office to office, or in boardrooms. Some told personal vignettes about their own experiences, while others related corporate stories, like John Deere's reluctance to put farmers out of business during the Depression. It was leadership by example at all levels of the company, where the culture exemplified the values, making it an understood way of conducting business. The company occasionally reinforced the corporate value system through statements in various internal communications, but it was more typically emphasized over time through an evolution of the culture.

But as John Deere grew in the late 1950s and early 1960s under the leadership of Bill Hewitt—employing almost 40,000 by 1964—it became apparent to leadership that as the company expanded in North America and throughout the world and more employees were hired, making clear, formal statements of how business should be conducted was essential to maintaining John Deere's culture in the future. For many years, blue bulletins—typed newsletters printed on blue paper—were the main means of companywide internal communications. Blue bulletins were the forum for announcing promotions, new positions, occasional corporate statements, and even birthdays.

E.F. "Woody" Curtis was president of John Deere in the

mid-1950s and at the request of Hewitt, he worked for several years devising the best means of making statements of corporate position to all John Deere employees. Drafts were passed back and forth among Curtis, company treasurer Joseph Dain, and Hewitt, before they ultimately decided in the early 1960s that blue bulletins would be used for ongoing departmental communications and a new format—Green Bulletins—would be used to clearly establish corporate policy and values to employees. Green Bulletins were to be issued sparingly, emphasizing the importance of content, and only by the John Deere chairman or chief executive officer.

The first John Deere Green Bulletin was issued by Hewitt in the summer of 1964, coinciding with the opening of the company's new administrative center. His remarks to employees in explaining the need for the Green Bulletin series still apply to the company 40 years later. "It is fitting that the first of these new bulletins be issued at this particular time," Hewitt told employees:

> On the one hand, the opening of the Deere & Company Administrative Center symbolizes the great progress made by the entire organization in recent years and emphasizes the rapid changes and increasing complexity that characterize the business economy today.
>
> On the other hand we are engaged in a major effort to establish the leadership of the John Deere name overseas. . . . Therefore, it seems particularly important that in the midst of change we should emphasize as clearly as we can and rededicate ourselves to the store of wisdom—

tried, tested and proven—accumulated by the men who built and steered the John Deere organization through these many years. It was their guide and remains as their legacy. It must live in our daily work and be increased by our efforts.

Hewitt told employees before outlining "basic principles" to be followed that although it had never been the John Deere practice to make formal statements of policy, clearly establishing principles that *should be used when making policies* was imperative. In stating the principles, he told John Deere employees dictums such as *business must be based on products and services for which the economy is willing to pay a premium*, the company *must make a profit*, it *must grow to the limits of its abilities*, and *mutual advantage is "the soundest basis" for each relationship* entered into by the organization.

Hewitt ended the Green Bulletin by emphasizing to employees the principle he viewed as the most important. "Integrity and merit are the bases of our continued success as an organization and as individuals within it," Hewitt wrote. "Of what do integrity and merit consist?"

COURTESY in every word.
HONESTY in every transaction.
DIGNITY in every personal act.
PROGRESSIVENESS in every thought.
CONSTRUCTIVENESS in every criticism.
QUALITY in every piece of work produced.

Additions to the Green Bulletin series were distributed to John Deere employees by Hewitt in 1966 and again in 1975, emphasizing such John Deere organizational practices as decentralization—*"the extent to which we put this concept into practice is a measure of our continuing ability to excel against our many competitors"*—and product quality and reliability. When Robert Hanson succeeded Hewitt in 1982 during the onset of economic recession, he re-issued the original Green Bulletin series with minor modifications to reflect changes in the company and its practices. Hans Becherer did the same in the 1990s, but both times, sections on John Deere's core values were left virtually untouched from the original drafting in 1964.

When corporate scandals hit at the turn of the twenty-first century following the grow-at-all-costs approach of the 1990s, some of the most trusted and valued companies in America suffered publicly due to questionable business practices and decisions. Even though John Deere's values-based decisions may have seemed dated at the time, the time-honored approach to conducting business the right way, regardless of trends of the moment, paid off when the go-go nineties yielded to a conservative business mindset of the new decade. Many John Deere employers, shareholders, and customers were happy that the company's culture had not let it stray from the manner in which business had been conducted for a century and a half.

"Our adherence to these values and the Green Bulletin

made us thankful when the scandals hit and we saw how some corporate business was modeled," said Mike Orr. "We were just doing it the only way we know how."

When Bob Lane reissued the Green Bulletins in August 2004, they contained more contemporary messages and wording but were built around the same emphasis on John Deere values. Lane also authored a personal, handwritten note to each member of the 250-person leadership team encouraging them with observations about how the Green Bulletins applied in their work and stressing the importance of maintaining the values of the company. Additionally, his announcement of the 12-bulletin series emphasized the word *how*.

"When I distributed the updated Green Bulletin series first to our global leadership team," Lane said, "I told them that just one word was underlined in my letter. Many immediately looked to see what it was. They understand, what's important is *how* we get it done."

- "Steadfast commitment to our core values is further expressed by the fact that we measure our accomplishments by *how* we achieve them as well as by the results themselves."
- "We are evaluated on what we accomplish, and on *how* we achieve these results."
- "*How* we measure value goes beyond immediate business results."
- "*How* we as employees carry out our individual responsibilities is as important as the success we achieve."

A LEVEL PLAYING FIELD

Lane moves easily at John Deere's headquarters and company facilities among employees, the highest ranking officer showing he does not value himself more than he values them. A visitor arriving early one day catches him sitting at an assistant's desk picking up a telephone call. At a company cocktail party, he excuses himself from a group of managers to refresh his own drink, water with a lime. At meetings for John Deere's worldwide leadership team, he sits on the front row, watching all presentations from fellow executives, and taking notes.

He understands his calling, to lead the company, and he values it, pushing with an intense conviction, but does not believe one person should be viewed as more important than others, whether it involves customers, employees, dealers, or shareholders. Lane talks directly and honestly to all about expectations, asking for the same in return. It's a cornerstone of integrity, he says, that is critical to John Deere's success. No talking in circles or with vague analysis of problems to please the chairman. Lane wants to know bad news early and thrives on the beauty of what he calls "high-performance teamwork" in which integrity is a springboard to meeting unified goals.

As a result, frankness is encouraged in problem solving at John Deere so fellow employees don't waste time trying to sift through incomplete responses, because speaking honestly is considered to be speaking with integrity. At John Deere, everyone seated around a table knows the other one "is playing with a full deck" with input, allowing the group to harness the power and exponentially move forward. "It's tough to make good decisions," said former chairman Hans Becherer. "But the quality of our decisions is what distinguishes John Deere."

Increasingly, companies everywhere have to explain to shareholders and consumers what they stand for in this age of corporate accountability that followed the greedy, go-go 1990s, proving they are more than just a machine for spitting out quarterly results. At John Deere, integrity has been a core value since its founding, but Lane is reinforcing it with vigor as the company pushes forward to achieve status as a great business. It's more important now, perhaps, than ever before, but it has little to do with the flavor of the moment in American business. Instead, it has everything to do with the John Deere way.

"The underlying value system is one of the keys to John Deere's longevity," said Mike Orr. "It all starts with John Deere and his commitment to doing it right. He made a powerful statement.

"The company today is doing business in different ways than it was in the beginning," Orr said. "But the thing that is untouchable is *how* we do business. Bob Lane never gives a talk without talking about the values of the company. He knows how important it is that we never lose that."

Lane is reinforcing integrity with vigor as the company pushes forward to achieve status as a great business. It's more important now, perhaps, than ever before, but it has little to do with the flavor of the moment in American business. Instead, it has everything to do with how John Deere has conducted business from the very beginning.

CHAPTER FIVE

Commitment Never Quits

JOHN DEERE WAS ALREADY EMBARKING ON GLOBAL EXPANSION in the mid-1950s when the opportunity arose to enter Western Europe through the purchase of a respected agricultural manufacturer. Already in Mexico and planning to enter South and Central America with fledgling operations, Chairman Bill Hewitt knew John Deere would best succeed in West Germany and other agriculturally-advanced European countries with a formidable entry into the marketplace instead of starting from scratch as a startup. As a result, the John Deere board of directors authorized the company in 1956 to purchase controlling stock (51 percent) of Heinrich Lanz, a well-known tractor and implement manufacturer based in Mannheim, West Germany, for $5.3 million.

John Deere had looked at purchasing Lanz in 1953, but the board ultimately had shot the proposition down, believing the European company's rapidly weakening position due primarily to its outdated tractor products would be a risky investment. Founded in 1859 by Heinrich Lanz, the German company specialized in harvesting equipment in the late 1800s and by the 1930s controlled more than 40 percent of the tractor market in its home country behind the sales strength of its inexpensive, single-cylinder Lanz Bulldog.

After World War II, Lanz struggled. Its facilities had been badly damaged during the war and its single-cylinder products were not competitive enough for the developing market, which required more power. The Lanz name was respected throughout West Germany, however, and its employees were noted for a John Deere-ish attitude in the workplace. That was enough for Hewitt and the board the second time they looked at acquiring the West German company, so in 1956 John Deere leaped into Europe with energy, enthusiasm, and the commitment to become a major competitor in the European agricultural market. The company from Moline, Illinois, became a true global manufacturer.

STAND BEHIND THE PRODUCT—AT ALL COSTS

The only problem was that John Deere did not enter Europe with the right products. Continuing with the single-cylinder Lanz was considered to be a mistake, since the product was not as strong as John Deere's two-cylinder tractor and had been viewed as outdated for years. And, although the German company had been working with production of its own four-cylinder tractor, the product was not up to John Deere's quality standards, so the decision was made to take U.S.-designed products and build them in West Germany. But the tractor John Deere sold in Europe as its full-size product was its utility tractor for North America. European farmers used the utility-sized tractor for full-size work, resulting in excessive breakdowns and warranty nightmares for the company.

Worsening the situation, John Deere's diesel engines were not as developed at the time as competitive European products, and its dealer organization was also not as developed as it was in North America, presenting the company with new challenges not faced before. Adding to the problems was the simple fact that John Deere's American-designed tractors were often too heavy and too slow for European farmers, who still face different conditions from farmers in the United States.

In Europe, for example, large farms are typically pieced together because of the fact that land was split up and sold centuries ago. For one farmer to have enough land to work to earn a living, he has to buy or lease smaller tracts of land in a bigger area, requiring tractors to spend far more time traveling on developed roads at higher speeds than in America. European agriculture is also far more intensive, because with less land, they are required to deliver more production. To obtain a yield four times higher per acre than a farmer from the United States, a German farmer has to work his land harder, dealing with more residue and slower speeds in the field.

For John Deere, it was in many ways the wrong product at the right time. Still, the company grew slowly in market share and earned some profit in Europe, which was not easy against strong competitors, including Massey-Ferguson and International Harvester, which were more developed in the region at the time. But John Deere was challenged in its core value of commitment because providing the service and backing the warranties on tractors that were being used beyond the limits of their original design was painful and costly.

It took more than 20 years for John Deere to get the right products built in Western Europe and develop a dealer base that reflected its strong and loyal presence in North America. It was not until 1989, when John Deere launched its new, European-designed tractor, that the world's largest maker of agricultural equipment hit the right product at the right time in Europe, but it made all the difference. The company's market share of tractor business in the region was 9 percent at the time, but grew steadily during the 1990s.

Under Bob Lane in 2001, the company launched dozens of additional new products in Europe designed specifically for the market. By 2004, John Deere was the fastest growing manufacturer of agricultural equipment in Western Europe, commanding 21 percent of the tractor business market share. Additionally, John Deere (12 percent) moved closer to major competitors CNH (17 percent) and AGCO (15 percent) in total market share of all agricultural equipment sold in Western Europe.

"We paid through the nose for many years in Europe," said former John Deere chairman Hans Becherer, "but we backed it up with the customers because we had given our word on the product. We did whatever we had to do because that was our promise. When we finally got it right, they appreciated our integrity and stayed with us. That stick-to-itiveness—we'll get it right even if it takes us twenty years—made a difference."

THE STRENGTH OF THE DEALER NETWORK

In North America, stories of John Deere sticking by its product date back generations and have been told and retold in communities all over, including places like Weiner, Arkansas; Peoria, Illinois; and Pennington, New Jersey. Typically, the product originates from factories to specification, but problems, of course, occur on occasion. It is the nature of manufacturing. But long before warranties became industry standard, John Deere let customers know that its commitment extended far beyond the equipment sales transaction. This means that any problems with products will not be ignored and that products will be ably and capably serviced and repaired throughout life cycles.

"People believe Deere will stand behind the product," said John Deere executive Sam Allen, "because they have seen us do it year after year. There are so many stories that have been told through the years. That permeates. You hear it and say, well, that's the John Deere way."

It's a difference maker for John Deere, particularly in its Agricultural Equipment division. Farmers have limited times when the seasons are right for planting and harvesting. If a tractor or combine needs service, they don't have time to wait in the heat of the moment while it sits idle, waiting for repair. Downtime is costly and stressful, making John Deere's core value of commitment as important as its core value of quality. How the company shows its commitment to customers on an ongoing basis is through its independent dealer network, numbering almost 1,600 agricultural equipment locations throughout North America.

When Bob Bodensteiner first joined the agricultural equipment business, it was not with John Deere. After graduating from college, he began working in Iowa as a salesman for a J.L. Case company-owned store in the small town of Decorah.

Five years later, he was managing a J.L. Case company-owned store near Davenport, Iowa. A John Deere dealer tried to hire him as a salesman, but young Bodensteiner said he was only interested in an equity position. He was offered, and accepted, a partnership in a dealership located near Fort Atkinson, Iowa, in 1977. "I was concerned about the future Case had in the farm equipment business," he said.

Three years later, Bodensteiner and his partner bought a small John Deere dealership in Clermont, Iowa—a tiny town of just 600 residents. When his partner left the business due to difficulties caused by the severe agriculture recession that had begun in the early 1980s, Bodensteiner got for a small investment his own John Deere dealership. At first glance, though, it was hardly a prize. Clermont was a hard-core farming community, but its size cast doubt over its business potential. The small town essentially had only a farm cooperative and a few other small businesses. The John Deere dealership was located in an old, aging downtown location and the facilities "looked terrible."

Times were difficult in farming. Prime interest rates in the 1980s were "running wild." Farmers were losing operations as land used as collateral could no longer be afforded. To try to keep dealerships open, John Deere made huge concessions across the board, forgiving interest and allowing dealers to pay for equipment only when it was sold to a customer. It was not enough, however, as the company still lost some key dealers in Iowa during the height of the recession. One casualty was a John Deere location Elkader, Iowa, just 20 miles from Bodensteiner's Clermont dealership. Elkader was a much larger town and its dealership had better facilities than Bodensteiner's Clermont store.

A John Deere territory manager suggested Bodensteiner close his shop, moving operations to Elkader. He had no interest in walking away from Clermont, however, where he had developed customer relationships and a surviving business. In 1985, the company allowed him to operate both, helping him get into the Elkader store at a low entry cost. The idea was that he would quickly see the strength of the Elkader location and move his operations there.

Within a couple of years, the farm recession eased and business at both locations improved. Bodensteiner modernized the Clermont store in the early 1990s and bought the property in Elkader. Another dealership became available in Decorah, his former home, and Bodensteiner bought it as well, becoming a multiple dealer at a time when most John Deere dealerships were single, one-store family operations. To effectively manage the business, Bodensteiner and his key employees at the different locations developed practices that would streamline operations at multiple locations and still maintain the John Deere, personal-service characteristics that customers had come to know and expect. In back office operations, uniform accounting procedures were put in place and policies were developed for making price quotes and for determining how much inventory to hold at each site. In customer service, Bodensteiner worked to continue to strengthen relationships with customers at each location. When farmers come into the store, he tries to get out and talk to them.

"One farmer," Bodensteiner said, "came in and said

to me, 'Give me a feel-good talk today.' I gave him one, because that's what he wanted and that's what he needed."

The strength of Bodensteiner Implement Company, though, is undoubtedly its commitment to providing service to customers at its four locations when needed. Anybody, Bodensteiner said, can make a price quote on a new equipment sale. And farmers, he said, are the "most competitive people I know," meaning that they are skilled at obtaining multiple quotes and driving for the best value. But when it comes to service, farmers quickly recognize where to turn because they can't afford downtime during peak seasons. Bodensteiner Implement, for instance, opens its service department 11 hours a day, six days a week during planting and harvest seasons, and parts are always available on Sundays. In fact, during harvest season, Bodensteiner Implement Company customers can order parts on Saturday and have them delivered to the farm on Sunday. Such commitment strengthens relationships and often parlays to the sales floor and to all other areas of the business.

"I tell our people," Bodensteiner said, "if our customer is down, it's our fault. If they are not running, it's our fault. When a customer's equipment is broken down and he has that deer in the headlights look, you want to be the one he goes to. You must be the 'go-to' place. It does not take [farmers] long to figure out where that is."

Multiple-location dealerships run by area owner–operators worked so well for John Deere in the 1990s that the company began to embrace consolidation of its franchised locations in regionalized areas. As a result, there are now drastically fewer

John Deere dealer–owners, but the dealerships are much stronger because they have greater business capacity and therefore can offer customers better service. The dealership contraction mimics changes in agriculture, where farmers are fewer, but their operations are bigger and more efficient.

A key to success for John Deere is that while it has actively supported dealer consolidation, it has worked to keep hands-on involvement from area owner–operators, maintaining, if not strengthening, the company's reputation for personal customer service. It is not conglomerations owning dealerships as you find in the auto business. Instead, it is local business people desiring to expand and serve larger areas. One such dealer is Marshall Stewart of Wynne, Arkansas. From a family with an agriculture background, Stewart did not return to Northeast Arkansas after college, pursuing a corporate career instead. But when the opportunity arose in 1999 to join a John Deere dealership in Wynne as a managing partner, he jumped at the chance to return to the area and business he knew and loved.

Coinciding with John Deere's desire to regionally consolidate dealerships, Stewart's return to Wynne as president of Greenway Equipment signaled the beginning of fast growth in the area. The dealership group rapidly acquired new locations and by the end of 2004 served John Deere customers in such fertile Arkansas farming grounds as Blytheville, Joiner, Hickory Ridge, Monette, Newport, Weiner, Wynne, Augusta, Des Arc, and Earle. Greenway Equipment had sales of more than $100 million and the business resembled nothing close to the mom-and-pop

John Deere dealerships of days gone by, except that the focus on the customer was as intense as ever before.

"It enables you to create economies of scale," Stewart said, "and actually provide the customer with better service. One of the problems in a single store environment is that during the harvest season, you might have 10 technicians. One month later, there might be just five, because there is not enough work for them.

"We tell our customers, we've got 80 technicians in the area," Stewart said. "If we decide to put a guy in a pickup truck and drive him 80 miles for service, that's our call and we will do that. It takes the peaks and valleys out of a cyclical business. Our business runs more efficiently and the customer gets more reliable service."

When Greenway acquires a new John Deere dealership, Stewart holds focus meetings in the community, telling customers how they can improve service. Greenway also asks for input specific to each location so they can meet and exceed expectations. "We alleviate fear of the unknown," Stewart said. "We are a bigger company [than customers had before], but we are still local in many ways, involved in their community and interested in building relationships."

Service is emphasized to the point during planting and harvest seasons where customers have contacts to call at all hours and days of the week, and decisions are often made with more regard for maintaining the long-term relationship than with regard for short-term profit. "We use the numbers for what they are," Stewart said. "But, we'll make business decisions at times that are not dollars and cents based. Sometimes, that ends up working to your benefit."

One example is when Greenway Equipment began allowing technicians to take service calls on Sundays. The idea was to let customers know they wanted to cover their bases at all times. Demand was high enough, though, that after-hours work became a profit source for the company. Now, it's standard policy that technicians are on call on Sunday. "We don't do things," Stewart said, "because that's how it's always been done. I don't have any preconceived notions. We try to run the business right, take care of customers, and change when necessary."

The Greenway story exemplifies the transition John Deere is orchestrating among its dealerships. Ownership becomes a more significant business organization, yet the community- and customer-based attitude remains.

A HOMETOWN REVIVAL

Commitment to the communities it serves has long been a practice at John Deere. When the company relocated its corporate headquarters in the 1960s to a campuslike setting on the outskirts of Moline, the downtown area of Deere's hometown languished for years with little identity or energy. It was a common problem in many other midsize U.S. communities—where urban sprawl left behind a downtown with no purpose. By the mid-1980s, Moline's downtown was spotted with empty warehouses, useless buildings, and an infrastructure that was no longer useful to the changing urban landscape. When the jobs left, so did the stores. Restaurants and retail operations moved to malls, also on the outskirts of town.

The Quad Cities boast more than 400,000 residents in the metropolitan area, but the municipal components making up the area are small, resulting in four individual downtown districts. Each suffered the same demise, as the land along both sides of the Mississippi River was unwanted despite the fact that it had once been home to thriving manufacturing and warehousing activity and evidence of the Quad Cities area's flowing lifeblood.

With a population of just 43,000, Moline's ailing commercial district cast a dark cloud on civic pride and caused deep concern for community leaders. John Deere still owned land and buildings in Moline's downtown, as well as the most significant piece of its economic history, dating back to 1848 when the founder had moved the company from Grand Detour 75 miles south to Moline on the banks of the Mississippi River.

Bob Hanson was John Deere chairman and CEO and his successor, Hans Becherer, was president of the company in 1987 when decisions were made to revitalize downtown Moline through detailed master planning and millions of public, private, and corporate dollars. It would be one of the most ambitious corporate-led downtown revitalization projects ever undertaken in a U.S. city of that size, and even though John Deere had significant operations elsewhere around the world, Moline was its home and the land along the river was viewed as its responsibility.

The timing was not great, considering John Deere had lost millions in 1987 and 1988 due to the poor farm economy, but downtown Moline, where the company had once been headquartered, where plows had once been built, and where a thriving local dealership once had stood, was in bad need of repair. "Stick-to-itiveness makes a difference," Becherer said. "We could not just walk away."

The project was complex even though it was in John Deere's hometown. The company's leadership initiated a layered planning process and determined that the revitalization would be a corporate project, taking advantage of multiple talents and divisions within the company. The John Deere Foundation was heavily involved, but it was more than just a civic helping hand. First Hanson, and then Becherer, was involved in planning and decision making on an ongoing basis, and many John Deere employees contributed to the project as part of their job. In 2002, Lane continued the company's commitment by authorizing the contribution of 20 acres of prime real estate owned by Deere for development by Western Illinois University.

Initially, John Deere created Renew Moline with the contribution of $100,000 and assistance with real estate expertise. The company also linked other corporations in the area to assist and tied in local politicians to create a true public–private partnership. Some resisted at first but ultimately saw it was in the community's best interest. The anchor of the project was The Mark of the Quad Cities civic arena, opened in the mid-1990s. Heavily funded by John Deere but not bearing the company's name, The Mark sits along the river and hosts major concerts, professional and college sports, and large conventions. The arena has for years been listed as one of the best venues of its size in the United States for selling out shows and bringing top-name attractions.

After years of work by private enterprise, concerned citizens, local, state, and federal politicians, and paid consultants, downtown Moline today is a tourist attraction that draws hundreds of thousands of visitors each year. In fact, outside of Chicago, the John Deere Pavilion—a center that includes the company's historic and current products and a wealth of interactive displays—is one of the most visited tourist spots in the state of Illinois. The Pavilion is part of an area known as the John Deere Commons, which is located on the same land that once was home to Deere's original Moline factory and headquarters. In addition to The Mark of the Quad Cities and the John Deere Pavilion, the Commons features an award-winning Radisson Hotel, a new office building that is home to a subsidiary of Deere, and the John Deere Store, which is packed full of merchandise and licensed products that visitors quickly buy to remember their stay in the hometown of the world's agricultural legend. The area around the Commons has seen a resurgence of restaurants, gift shops, and modern offices, as well as brand-new headquarters for the area's Red Cross organization—built on land donated by John Deere. The Mississippi River is now in view for visitors to enjoy, and nearby is a landing dock for a boat that shuttles tourists around the four-city area. In all, the development work has brought recognition as a model for private-public cooperation and has been emulated by others.

A final piece of the project for John Deere was the opening of the John Deere Collector's Center just two blocks away from its John Deere Pavilion. The center, funded in part through a state grant obtained by the John Deere Foundation, is a re-creation of a 1950s-era dealership, displaying antique Deere tractors and farm equipment. The collector's center caters to the enthusiast and complements the nearby Commons, bringing more tourists to downtown Moline. The revitalization has been contagious, as more businesses and restaurants have moved into the area, and now other Quad Cities municipalities are working toward or considering similar revitalization efforts.

The problem with local leadership, of course, is that it always gets heavily leaned on. As manufacturing left the area, so did a lot of corporate community assistance. As the largest employer in the Quad Cities, the John Deere Foundation gets pulled in every direction. It gives each year locally, handsomely, but is expanding its commitment, now that much of the work is done in restoring Moline, to other areas served by John Deere.

COMMITMENT TO THE PRODUCT

If you drive up to parking lots adjoining manufacturing facilities of the world's largest automakers, typically roughly half of the cars parked in the lot are made by the company that operates the plant. Workers may have loyalty to their employer, but the desire for diversity gives way to a home-team sellout when it comes to purchases. A Nissan worker wants to drive a Ford; a Ford worker wants to drive a Nissan. At John Deere, you will rarely find a company employee anywhere using competitive products when a green machine is available to do the same job. It's the ultimate commitment of the people, who steadfastly support John Deere products as the company's most steadfast customers.

Bob Lane, for instance, might be seen in his driveway

early on a cold winter morning just after a Midwestern snow-
fall blowing snow from his driveway with a John Deere snow
blower. And when his wife, Patty, interviewed a lawn service
to tend to the couple's Moline yard, the last question she
asked the apparent hired helper after the interview was
whether he owned and operated John Deere mowers. The
answer was no. She interviewed again, this time with a
larger lawn service. They promised to do a good job, but
they did not use John Deere products. Patty e-mailed her
husband, wondering if they should use the service.

"Absolutely not," Bob Lane said.

The lawn service bought a John Deere lawn tractor and
got the job.

"I'm usually not so firm in such instances," Lane said,
"but when it involved a job a John Deere product can do,
and perform better, there was no other consideration."

You'd expect company executives to be especially loyal to
their brand. At Deere, some executives even require home-
builders that construct their residences to use only John Deere
equipment. But even more impressive is when someone lower
in the organizational chart makes the same kind of demand of
suppliers. In the 1990s, the company's managed health care
subsidiary was constructing a building when a contractor
showed up to work on the site with a competitor's equipment.
The mid-level manager told the supplier that this was a John
Deere building being built on John Deere land with funds
from John Deere sales and he wouldn't expect that any contractor who was benefiting from John Deere would do work in
this situation with anything but a Deere.

Just as insightful is the movement in some cities where

Deere has a large manufacturing presence by employees to pressure their local city councils to dub the town a "John Deere community" and require their public works and parks departments to only buy John Deere equipment.

COMMITMENT TO THE COMPANY

The stories of commitment that circulate at John Deere are numerous. They could literally fill thousands of pages. Most involve customers talking about the longevity of their purchases, or about how the company backs up its product, or about dealers providing unusual, personal service. One that typifies the John Deere experience and the commitment that results from ongoing business relationships belongs to Art Van Camp of Mississauga, Ontario, Canada.

As a young, twenty-something-aged man in Canada 30 years ago, Van Camp heard that a company named Deere was looking to expand its construction equipment dealership base in his area. Van Camp knew about John Deere and its reputation for quality and believed a dealership was a perfect business opportunity. He asked for a meeting with a territory manager. Van Camp told him he had little to no money and no experience selling construction equipment. The John Deere representative was not encouraging during the meeting, but he agreed to meet Van Camp again. This time, Van Camp convinced him that his aggression and hunger to succeed would serve Deere well.

He got a construction equipment dealership and started in business with just $28,000 in the bank. The company financed the equipment on his lot and financed many of his startup costs. "They set me up," Van Camp said. "I told them what I could do and they committed to me all along the way."

In return, he worked hard to build relationships with customers, trying to fill gaps that Caterpillar and others had missed. His business was successful until a painful recession hit in the 1980s. Equipment worth millions sat on his lot, yet Deere did not make him pay interest. The figure, he said, would have put him out of business. When the recession ended, his business thrived again and when the company began seeking consolidation in the construction business, he was asked to join others in Ontario and expand his territory through one, unified dealership.

ONTRAC was formed after four Ontario dealerships merged, making the Mississauga-based company one of the largest John Deere dealerships in North America. ONTRAC now has 14 locations in Ontario after acquiring other independent dealers and their subsidiary branches. Van Camp is president and a partnership owner of ONTRAC Equipment Services of Ontario, Canada. The company generated equipment sales of more than $300 million in 2003.

"Most of us started out as smaller mom-and-pop dealers," Van Camp said, "and they propped us up and supported us and showed us the potential. They've stuck with me all the way. Anybody that knows me will tell you, I love that company because of what they've allowed me to do."

The experience of Art Van Camp is similar to those of many others who have had John Deere relationships and experiences through the years. Whether they are dealers, suppliers, customers, or employees, the commitment from the company never quits.

CHAPTER SIX

Build a Business
as Great as Your Products

JOHN DEERE HAS LONG BEEN KNOWN FOR ITS GREAT PROD-
ucts. From tractors of all sizes to high-end combines to the
multiple-use Gator utility vehicle, owning one of the trademark green products stamped with the yellow leaping deer
logo means owning the premier equipment available in the
market. Nothing, after all, "Runs Like a Deere." But since
the largest part of John Deere's diversified business is manufacturing, a segment highly influenced by economic trends
and cycles, the company's business results have not always
been as great as its products. Buying a John Deere tractor,
for example, has been a no-lose proposition through the
years. It comes with the promise of quality and the commitment from the company and its dealers to see that it delivers to expectations.

But buying John Deere stock has through the years been
more of a roller coaster ride, typical of all companies viewed
on Wall Street as cyclical in nature. When the agriculture
business boomed, so did John Deere stock, riding at the high
end, worthy of the company's preeminent status in North
America. When the agriculture business suffered, so did

John Deere stock, taking the obligatory downswing as many investors wait for a cyclical bottom.

When Bob Lane took over as John Deere chairman and CEO in 2000, he recognized that the company's focus at the beginning of the twenty-first century should be on making John Deere's business as great as its products, which, if achieved, would reward customers, employees, and shareholders alike by making the company stronger, year after year. The idea was not to move away from areas that have made John Deere products great for so many years, like quality, design, and innovation, but to move forward in the tradition of John Deere leadership by taking the company's strengths of its past and adding on another vital component in the effort of making it stronger for the future.

For Lane, this vision of building a business as great as its products began immediately after he was appointed John Deere chief financial officer in 1997. He had a background in banking before joining John Deere in the 1980s and had significant responsibility with company finance in overseas responsibilities in the 1990s, but it was when he stepped into the office of CFO that he began clarifying the need for John Deere to strengthen its business and began saying from the first day on the job that the company would benefit long-term from lighter assets and wider margins. The company's roller-coaster ride at the end of the 1990s reinforced his idea that the business needed improvement to become as reliable as John Deere products.

The American stock market was in the middle of its boom period in 1998 and John Deere was experiencing record profits, posting the company's first year of $1 billion in profits. The company had grown its presence in the consumer lawn and turf care market, strengthened its position in construction equipment, broadened its credit operations, and expanded manufacturing operations globally in efforts to reduce some of the impact of cyclical swings, but when the U.S. agriculture business began another downturn in 1999, John Deere stock collapsed along with those of other equipment manufacturers while the rest of the stock market continued a frenzied upward run. The situation in heavy equipment got worse when the economic bubble began losing air in 2000, resulting in flat sales, production cutbacks, and reductions in working capital.

Hans Becherer's already-scheduled retirement took place in August of that year and Bob Lane took over at John Deere, faced with leading the company in difficult economic conditions further complicated by the impending burst of the American economic bubble. The setting was not too different from what Becherer had faced when taking over from Bob Hanson in 1989 following a prolonged and severe agricultural downturn in which John Deere had to shrink to survive. Becherer led the company back with its Genuine Value restructuring program, aimed at cutting costs and strengthening through independence among internal divisions. Genuine Value worked, as earnings and the Deere & Company stock price increased throughout most of the 1990s, but John Deere's business was suffering again as the new millennium approached and the agricultural business dipped yet again.

"The purchase of John Deere equipment, like most heavy equipment, is very cyclical," said chairman and CEO Bob

Lane. "We have great products. As a business, we have had great years. But our business results had not been like our products. . . . It has not been great year after year. That was one part of our company's DNA that needed to change."

Even in the good years, when John Deere made millions in profits at the height of strong cycles, the returns on company assets were less than they could or should have been. The focus was mostly on the amount of profits, not on how much the company had to spend to earn its profits.

"If someone told you he or she made ten dollars today on an investment," Lane said, "you might think that was good . . . a ten dollar profit. But the question to ask is if he or she made ten dollars' profit on a 100 dollar investment or if he or she made a ten dollar profit on a 1,000 dollar investment. One would be good, the other not so good."

The company had been using a return on assets (ROA) formula as the primary measurement for management's performance bonuses since the 1990s when Becherer had implemented the Genuine Value program that had cut costs and realigned the company into six strategic business units, making each independently responsible for contributions to the greater corporation. Additionally, the Construction and Forestry Equipment division introduced a program in the division in the late 1990s that was similar to Economic Value Added (EVA), a model developed by consultants Stern Stewart and Company, which measures the true economic profit of an enterprise by taking net operating profit after taxes and subtracting capital used times the cost of capital to obtain EVA. Managers were reluctant to adopt the new financial measure, but division leadership persisted.

Since Deere & Company is a decentralized corporation, the same measures were not implemented in every division. As a result, the entire company was operating under the same general standards but the results continued to vary. When times were tough during cyclical downturns, John Deere's return on its assets was far more negative than what the company gained during the good years. Nevertheless, the concept of comparing profits to the cost of capital was not a new focus for company leadership. In John Deere's first Green Bulletin series, chairman Bill Hewitt wrote that profit is "the ultimate test of business performance" and "the basic necessity of business success is to operate in such a manner that after paying all costs and expenses there is left sufficient compensation in the form of a profit which is commensurate with the amount of capital used and the degree of risk run."

As a whole, however, the mindset of the company through the years was to invest, to build, and to sell good products, judging the quality of profits solely on quantity, not return. "We were doing business," Lane said, "in very expensive ways."

A NEW WAY OF THINKING

To create change, Lane went straight to John Deere's strength, its worldwide employees, and gave the culture steeped in tradition a daunting challenge. The company that had existed for generations with less instead of more when it came to human resources mandates would unveil one of the most comprehensive performance management systems used in companies today. The idea is to provide every single one of John Deere's salaried employees with an individual online job performance outline that includes an updated assessment with each directly linked to short- and long-term business strategy goals. It was fine to have decentralized operating divisions where decisions in the field could be made swiftly and effectively to serve customers and obtain quality, but Lane knew that employees around the world, all working for the common corporate good, must have common objectives.

"It has been part of the culture for employees to come to work for John Deere and to stay for 30 or more years," Lane said. "Most were not getting evaluated and almost none were being judged against predetermined criteria."

The objective was unveiled in June 2000, during his first meeting with John Deere's worldwide leadership group. During Lane's entire address before the group, which is made up of the company's top 200 managers, the backdrop on the stage behind him was a nonchanging slide that showed just one number. The audience of company leaders, curious about what message their new chief executive would deliver in his first appearance before the group, wondered about the significance of the number — 18,000. Ultimately, Lane revealed this was the number of John Deere salaried employees at the time and that each would be a part of a new employee Global Performance Management System that would be the backbone of a strategy to make John Deere's business as great as its products, not only for customers and employees but also for shareholders.

"The company's product," Lane said, "became the benchmark because for John Deere, our products have always been exceptional. With human resources performance, we have to have the same high standard."

Lane knew the Global Performance Management System would be controversial inside a company that had never experienced such a dramatic addition to its human resources strategy, so he initially placed in charge an individual from the operating divisions who was already highly respected for his management skills in several of John Deere's largest manufacturing operations. To ensure that performance management became a distinct part of the culture, the system's introduction required the same rigor as is needed to build a quality John Deere tractor.

H.J. Markley, who is now one of two presidents in the

How to Run Like a Deere

- **Run Smart**

  Tell employees to "think like an inventor" and use appropriate technology to find new ways to solve customers' problems and use the most efficient processes to quickly get those into customers' hands.

- **Run Fast**

  Tell employees to "think like a customer" quickly to provide products and services customers can use.

- **Run Lean**

  Tell employees to "think like an investor," which means getting high returns, using assets efficiently, and eliminating activities that don't help achieve high enough margins.

company's Agricultural Equipment division, was put in charge of implementing John Deere's Global Performance Management System. Markley had served as general manager of the company's Dubuque and Waterloo facilities during a career that began in 1974 after he graduated with an MBA from the Amos Tuck School at Dartmouth College.

At two of the key manufacturing sites for the company, Markley had implemented and managed many processes that streamlined and helped perfect the building of heavy equipment. In manufacturing, support systems were in place to ensure high performance. Goals were set, problems identified, and resources appropriately deployed. However, in the world of employee performance management, the same could not be said. Indeed, most employees were dedicated to hard work, customer satisfaction, and quality products. But alignment was not certain. No system was in place to ensure this alignment took place. It was one part of the company's culture that needed to be addressed.

Deere CEO Bob Lane says he believes that human resources success is not peripheral but is at "the core of the core" in determining the long-term viability of an organization. To ensure that the performance management system was launched with great success, he felt a respected leader who had already managed sophisticated work processes already proving to be quite effective was needed.

By introducing the performance management system to company employees in terms that equated high-quality manufacturing results with consistency in work processes, Markley earned respect for the importance of the performance management system and helped most employees understand the benefit to the company and its long-term success.

CROSSING THE LINE

But Bob Lane's goals for the future of John Deere went beyond the people and the products. For John Deere to be considered a truly great company, he believed the business needed to become as great as the products. Shareholder value added (SVA) is the metric Lane unveiled at the meeting just three months after becoming chairman.

Lane announced that SVA, based on a simplified version of the economic value added formula used previously in the Construction and Forestry division, was a metric that operating staff worldwide could understand, and it would be implemented company-wide, with all employees working toward the common goal of producing increased shareholder value. Lane set lofty objectives, believing that to become a truly great business, John Deere needed to aim high.

The line was originally established at 12 percent to be acceptable on what the company referred to as operating return on operating assets (OROA). But to be a great business, Lane eventually concluded that John Deere actually needed to strive for a 20 percent annual OROA—a level better than the company's best year in its history.

Terms were explained easily, and Lane communicated often that the role of the 18,000 salaried employees was vital to getting the job done. Simply, operating return on operating assets (OROA) was the measure while shareholder value added (SVA) was the outcome—additional cash created from a more efficient operation using less assets. The engine of this new approach was considered to be the Global Performance Management System, aligning the high horsepower of dedicated employees to work on clear objectives. Lane said often that it meant setting aside what might be good to do for what would greatly impact the objective. The company targeted significant increases in SVA—the difference between the cost of capital and pretax profit—and Lane considered himself the cheerleader.

"The biggest job I have is to tell the story in a way that everyone understands and can support with their action on the job," Lane said.

Benefiting Deere in this effort to improve the business results was a significantly strong relationship with organized labor groups that represent some of the company's North American manufacturing employees. John Deere broke new ground in the 1990s when it negotiated a six-year labor agreement with the United Auto Workers, gaining union leadership's confidence over the term of the contract to sign another six-year pact in 2003.

Constant attention to providing a great workplace for manufacturing employees while also aligning high-performance teamwork with the salaried workforce became the formula for success at John Deere.

Shareholder Value Added measures what shareholders are earning with John Deere in comparison to what they could earn by investing elsewhere at similar risk.

"We're asset people," Lane said. "We understand machines, tires, receivables . . . assets. We decided to make this simple, in terms that we work with every day. I told everybody we needed aligned high-performance teamwork and that the mission was now being turned over to the people."

The goal was to begin reducing John Deere's larger assets first, including receivables and inventory. Receivables are made up mostly of money owed for machines that have been sold to dealers that they have not sold yet, and inventory is the equipment and materials used in the factories to build the machines and also excess machines that are built and stored but not yet shipped. By restructuring the business to get machines into the hands of customers as quickly as possible, assets and inventory are drastically reduced. It sounds simple enough. However, the company-wide commitment to SVA did not happen overnight.

Many managers steeped in John Deere's culture were slow to embrace the asset-based performance demands and some even spent more time debating about the unfairness rather than wholeheartedly embracing it. There were arguments that financial metrics should be division-based. Complicating the rollout was the fact that John Deere and other manufacturers were still mired in a depressed farm market. Further complications came when the general U.S. economy slumped as well. Conditions didn't seem perfect for making the company "Run Like a Deere."

The Global Performance Management System did not implement easily overnight, either. In the past, John Deere had not emphasized consistent documentation in job goals

The Three A's That Key Business Success

1. **Aspirations**
   Everyone must have a strong desire to perform on average better than the previous best.

2. **Alignment**
   If all company employees are aligned, the results will be awesome.

3. **Awards**
   Employees will receive job enrichment and monetary fulfillment awards for meeting and exceeding short-term, medium-term, and long-term objectives.

for employees, so creating a comprehensive and aligned system of goal setting for 18,000 employees was not easy. To outline expectations and goals, employees had to be more accountable to company objectives in their job performance. Adding to the pressure was a timeline for change that was considered short, based on the compact, structured plan to transform the company into a great business in just a few years.

The challenge for management was explaining the need for a high-performance environment and getting the employee culture to accept and embrace this change.

John Deere's Sam Allen, who was the company's executive in charge of global human resources in 2004, knew the work was worthy of the payoff.

"If we did not create the best environment for performance, we faced the potential that the best performers would leave for a better environment," he said.

Employees were told that tangible benefits were involved in embracing the change. As Lane says, employees like to win and they like to be justly rewarded for hard work and meeting and exceeding expectations. John Deere's "total rewards strategy" reconfigured several levels of variable pay to more directly reward high performance at every level of employment at the company. That means bonuses are not automatic simply because the business cycle is treating the company well. Shareholder value added must be delivered at all points of the business cycle for managers to benefit in the form of variable pay or what some know as performance bonuses. The bar is raised during high points in industry sales and makes the entire John Deere team focus more on running a great business consistently year to year. The opportunity exists to make more money in performance bonuses than in the past if the shareholder also gains through shareholder value added. Lane emphasizes that creating a product that pleases the customer and an environment in which people want to work are significant parts of the equation. In meeting those criteria responsibly, he has said, decisions that are made will also be in the interests of the company owners, the shareholders.

Ultimately, the change is making John Deere's human resources strategies contribute to the company's SVA as a catalyst of strong business performance. Sam Allen summarizes it best when he states, "Overall, the whole effort is built around the basic objectives of helping people be the best they can be, and keeping us all motivated and passionate about high performance and aligned teamwork."

To better emphasize the importance of the SVA plan to

John Deere's Three Keys to HR Success

- Strong leadership teams, meaning leadership at all levels of the company, who understand the business, make fast decisions, and inspire other employees.
- A Global Performance Management System that makes strategies and goals clear and makes it possible for employees to align their work with those goals.
- Assurance that employees feel empowered to continually learn and improve.

---

employees and explain more clearly the means of achieving the objectives, Lane introduced further layers of the first-phase SVA plan (2001–2004) six months after the leadership meeting in San Antonio designed to better articulate the mission of "crossing the line" of SVA return. He often uses slogans and catchy phrases so employees can better understand the mission. "If there's substance to them," he said, "you get a handle on what it is you are trying to achieve." To explain how the company would achieve its SVA goal, Lane's team worked with outside consultants to define the strategy and established objectives in three areas:

1. **Sprint North**—Achieve exceptional operating performance.
2. **Seed East**—Seek and establish disciplined SVA growth.
3. **Align Teamwork**—Link employees and divisions to common global enterprise goals.

IT IS BETTER TO BE LEAN THAN LADEN

When Lane looked at John Deere's assets ledger after taking over the company leadership in 2000, he saw a repetitive theme. The company was bogged down by heavy assets that did not provide a sufficient return to shareholders. Lane felt John Deere was laden by millions of dollars in investments that were not delivering adequate returns. Some businesses were profitable; others were not. Deere's team decided that some plants needed to be closed, machinery assets needed to be better managed, and an entire product line had to be sold. The company could not expect a reasonable return from these assets, so swift, albeit painful, action would be taken to alleviate the burden, or John Deere's business would continue underperforming for shareholders.

A subset of the Sprint North objective was Prune West, meaning if the business unit or product line could not meet financial criteria, it would have to be cut from the company's assets. As a result, John Deere announced a major restructuring in August 2001 designed to get rid of underperforming assets, cut costs, and create a stronger foundation for delivering increased SVA. A cornerstone of this plan was the sale of John Deere's Homelite brand consumer products business. Acquired in 1994, Homelite's standalone brand of chain saws and blowers had been a struggle for John Deere since the beginning, and the business had lost $70 million in 2000 on a pretax basis. Some estimates placed the loss several times that amount over the time that Deere owned the line. John Deere had acquired Homelite for noncyclical growth in the early 1990s but had found that even though the brand was established and known, it did not have the same consumer power as John Deere. The business was no longer a good fit for John Deere, and Homelite was sold in 2001 to TechTronics Industries of Hong Kong.

Some of the moves, however, were much more painful and severe than the traditional asset sale. John Deere built a new, state-of-the-art, $38 million, 300,000-square-foot manufacturing facility in the Tennessee Great Smoky Mountains in 1999 to build skid steer loaders, the generic name for what many people know as the Bobcat—which happens to be the most popular brand in the product category. Known for its advanced manufacturing systems, the plant produced John Deere's commercial skid steer loaders and employed roughly 250 nonunion workers.

Another manufacturing plant, in Virginia, was in a similar situation. Deere had constructed it to exclusively build its utility vehicles. But these assets weighed heavily on John Deere's balance sheet. Lane made the call, closing the new facilities to return the work to unionized factories that had built John Deere products for generations, to employees dedicated to John Deere quality, to locations that appeared to have more production capacity than was currently being used.

"Some [investments] were new and modern and it was a pity," said Nate Jones, chief financial officer, "but we could not sprint North with them and we could not rationalize keeping them."

Additional actions saw John Deere reduce its U.S. salaried workforce by 8 percent, cut back equipment production to more quickly reflect changes in consumer demand cycles, and restructure the divisions to optimize employment levels and overall costs. "These actions," Jones said, "send a clear signal that we are not content to simply wait for the economy to improve in order to make our business more profitable."

Deere & Company reported a net loss of $64 million for the 2001 fiscal year, including one-time write-offs, down from a $486 million profit in 2000. More importantly, the company had a negative enterprise SVA result of $1.2 billion as the plan to reduce assets and deliver higher returns kicked in. To emphasize its importance and the urgency of its execution, Lane wrote a letter to the same John Deere worldwide leadership group he had addressed the year before when announcing the new objectives. Dated November 30, 2001, the letter suggests that over a long period of time the company had "delivered relatively poor financial performance, despite our great products, people and market position.

"Even more concerning," Lane wrote, "our financial results have lagged not only in recessionary times, but also in the best of times. We must change this performance."

Included in the letter was a chart that compared SVA returns in John Deere's equipment operations business from 1991 through 2001. "When you look at the chart, you will see a sobering reality," Lane wrote. "Although it is clear that progress was being made, in the end only '97 and '98—out of the last 11 years—were close to being adequate. If we are to be a great business, the worst years must be close to zero, and the normal years will have to be better than even our best year of 1997."

Lane continued, talking about John Deere's committed employees, its unique heritage, and the unparalleled products known around the world for quality and reliability. But, Lane said, John Deere must overcome two major shortcomings:

1. "We are asset heavy, meaning that in the equipment business we use more inventory, receivables, and plant equipment than necessary to serve customers well.
2. We are margin deficient because we spend too much, and we do not always adequately design and charge for the value our customers define and desire."

Many problems with the business are typical of older manufacturing companies where tradition becomes standard practice for so long that standing back to identify trouble is hard enough. Fixing the problems seems out of the question. An example is in John Deere's larger segment of business, combines. "These are great products," Lane said. "They are factories on wheels . . . you have crops and within five minutes you have this clean grain, all done on the go."

But John Deere's combine business was operating similarly to the auto industry where the ultimate goal is to keep factories running and get product out the door. Dealers received cozy finance terms, allowing them to take back old equipment and sell new ones without having a home for the old. While the dealer worked at selling the old combine, it sat on the lot interest free, taking profits off the top of the new combine. Often the new combine went out the door with a less-than-inviting incentive. Even in boom cycles, John Deere's top-of-the-line agriculture business did not deliver the returns it should have. The whole process was in need of repair. When Lane met with the agriculture dealers at their annual meeting in 2002, he announced that such financing arrangements must stop so John Deere and its dealers could escape the endless cycle. Combines would be built to order and sold at fair margins, and dealers should look for buyers for the used equipment first.

"I tell everybody the same story," Lane said. "We told our dealers we were going to build a better business. If they couldn't support our plans, it was time for them to make a change. But in creating a great business, in the long run, we would also be helping their business of representing a great company."

WHY BE A GREAT BUSINESS?

The question is obvious. When a company has survived as long as John Deere, evolving from its beginning in 1837 as a Midwest manufacturer of plows into a multibillion dollar, global manufacturer of some of the world's most respected equipment, a natural tendency is to wonder why the business would need to be repaired in the first place.

"The author Thomas Friedman said that any corporation that is not superb in today's environment will become road kill in today's globalization," Lane said. "We at John Deere do not have a divine right to continue succeeding as our predecessors had. No company in the agricultural equipment industry has survived intact over the past 20 years except John Deere. All the others have consolidated."

The idea to build a great business was not one based on

the concept of hollowing out the business with cuts and a short-term view. Rather, the plan is to reward shareholders with long-term growth. To do so, Lane said, "the game must be played on the field since shareholders can't be served directly. We have to deliver on a more consistent basis to the ones who provide us money—the customers. In doing this in combination with lean asset management, we will benefit the shareholder.

"We will not compromise our integrity," Lane said. "So, if you think about it, enduring performance for shareholders is possible only if performance for customers and employees is superb and sustained. In fact, without performing to the exacting high standards set by our chosen customers and without being an employer of choice for the finest employees, it is simply impossible to sustain our historic values and the level of performance year after year to which we aspire for our shareholders."

If we don't improve our business, we'll be a division of someone else.

—Robert W. (Bob) Lane,
John Deere chairman and CEO

The idea, Lane said, is to hold onto John Deere's values outlined in the Green Bulletin series, while achieving the aspirations of becoming a great business. In the end, he said, the winners are shareholders, who are rewarded with higher returns; customers, who benefit from a more stable, enduring company; and employees, who have the potential for higher monetary rewards for consistently high performance.

"We've always pushed," Lane said, "but we've pushed for

five to seven yards every play. If that's what we got, fine. But now, we want first downs and we want first downs every time."

To illustrate the benefits of using the value returned to shareholders as a primary guide of business, he likes to use the four cardinal virtues of humans—fortitude, temperance, prudence, and justice—as models for why companies like John Deere should aspire to create value for shareholders in the short and long term.

VIRTUE EQUALS LONG-TERM SUCCESS

Virtues alone are not sufficient for prosperity, Lane said, but they are necessary for sustaining it. Ultimately, as the corporation sustains its performance and endures, "it can contribute to human flourishing by providing goods and services that add value to the quality of life, an honorable way to make a living, the potential for wealth generation for those willing to risk investment, and, through the paying of taxes, direct support of public and social needs."

Sustained Value Creation Requires Fortitude

John Deere could deliver greater short-term results for investors by drastically cutting research and development, but in the long run the company would suffer by pulling away from its core value of innovation. The plan is not to sacrifice the future, but rather to ensure that John Deere becomes a great business that continues on the strength of great products and lasting customer relationships.

Sustained Value Creation Requires Temperance

John Deere must show restraint as a corporation to sustain its performance, because when rational moderation turns into irrational excess, failure is imminent. For example, John Deere's business suffered periodically in the past because the company did not restrain its assets levels, allowing inventory and receivable levels to remain consistently and unnecessarily high.

Sustained Value Creation Requires Prudence

Prudence, or the ability to discern the most suitable and profitable course of action, is allowing John Deere manufacturing to operate in a more lean, efficient, and profitable manner. Lane uses the company's Construction and Forestry division as an example of how prudence can pay big dividends. In 1997, he said, the division manufactured almost 25 percent of its annual production each quarter, despite the fact that customer demand was seasonal, creating piles of inventory and excess cost during off-cycles. The company was laden with assets at times, while at other times customer needs could not be met fast enough due to limited supply. But prudent, leaner manufacturing has allowed John Deere's Construction and Forestry division to deliver products faster in demand cycles and reduce costs in down cycles.

Sustained Value Creation Requires Justice

For a company to sustain its performance, it must follow the ultimate virtue of justice, which sums up all the others. For John Deere, that means building the best products possible so the customer spending hard-earned money to make purchases is justly rewarded with the best the company can deliver. Additionally, justice must be provided to all the company has relationships with, including dealers and suppliers.

THE DIVIDENDS OF SUCCESS

Despite initial difficulty in adjusting to the Global Performance Management System and the SVA basis for gauging business success, progress was being made by 2002. Lane had personally visited almost every John Deere operational unit around the world, explaining the benefits of building a business as great as the company's products, and talking about the means of delivering more shareholder value and ultimately crossing the established return on assets line on each trip. The company's decentralized culture was finally migrating toward unified business standards and understanding the benefits of improving the business.

By the fourth quarter of fiscal year 2002 it showed, since Deere & Company posted a $68 million profit. For the year (2002) net income had rebounded to $319.2 million, a dramatic improvement over the $64 million loss in 2001. More importantly, SVA was closed to a negative $462 million in 2002, and in 2003 John Deere closed the SVA gap to a negative $33 million as the company earned net income of $643 million.

The work paid off in 2004, when the company's commitment to build a better business, combined with improving market conditions, led to John Deere significantly crossing the line for its targeted operating return on operating assets. John Deere delivered in excess of $1.4 billion in profits for the year (more than two times the previous year), and employees at all levels of the company, including unionized employees, were poised to benefit from bonuses linked specifically to performance. The company's stock, as a result, was trading at about $70 per share, compared with an average of $33 per share in August 2000.

To celebrate and transition to the next phase of the business strategy, Lane gathered the company's worldwide leadership group together for a meeting in the Quad Cities area in fall 2004 for the first time since they had met during his first days in office as CEO in 2000. By not holding any meeting of the entire group since then, Lane had not interrupted their pursuit of the daunting task of creating a better business. Now, in 2004, the company's top 250 global leaders gathered, meeting for three days, sharing with one another what they had done to cross the line and what might create challenges for remaining on the line and creating more growth in the future.

At the end of the first day of meetings, Lane called them all together for a dinner, in which he promised to toast three years of hard work resulting in John Deere crossing the line. The leaders sat together at tables, each holding a glass of 1970 French Bordeaux, poured from bottles aged in the wine cellar in the company's world headquarters. The cellar and the wine collection originated with former chairman Bill Hewitt, whose taste for art and fine wine is still legendary at John Deere. When the building opened in 1964, Hewitt was presented one key, said to open every door in the building—including the wine cellar. It has been passed along among his successors.

"I did some looking," Lane said, "and there is some 1970 Bordeaux in there, which I hear was a very good year." Normally saved for board meetings or smaller special occasions since the quality reserve is in small quantity, the wine was poured for 250 in recognition of what many thought a few years before would be impossible. "Why celebrate?" Lane said. "Because you've done extraordinary work and . . . because I inherited the key. Together, we toast crossing the line, and we thank Bill Hewitt for his foresight."

The quest for John Deere to become a great business was only the beginning, however. To be a great business, Lane said, the company must sustain its performance into the future. His challenge was to repeat the performance of returning value to the shareholders by meeting and exceeding the OROA targets for the next five years. Then the company can toast once again, enjoying the benefits of endurance. "If we are going to be a great business," Lane said, "it will take five years to illustrate that this is something that is sustaining and enduring. Five years from now, I hope to declare we are a great business."

To accomplish the five-year objective, Lane unveiled during the leadership meeting the second phase of the business strategy, which now included growth, and slightly changed nomenclature—"Growing a Business as Great as Our Products." This is to be the purpose of John Deere beginning in 2005. Doing it one year is rewarding. Doing it five years means John Deere earns the right to be called a great business, and shareholders and employees will continue to be rewarded, particularly in performance during down cycle years when previously there was no hope of investment return or employees earning bonuses. New phrases were unveiled to illustrate the mission of crossing the growth line and sustaining performance:

- Sustain North for Preeminence
- Drive East for SVA Growth
- Aim High with Teamwork

"Why are we so focused on sustainable SVA as opposed to other measures?" Lane said. "SVA—basically the difference between operating profit and an implied pretax cost of capital—is the one metric that captures the benefits of asset discipline, bottom-line efficiency and customer-pleasing top-line growth. This is especially true when positive SVA is sustained over a period of years, which is certainly our aspiration."

This message is one Lane shares with everyone involved with John Deere, whether it is the leadership of the United Auto Workers, a John Deere dealer, a customer, an employee, or a community leader where Deere is present. He works to help them understand that even though John Deere's business mission is to serve shareholders, it's done through field level execution, meaning that John Deere must take care of customers and employees better than ever before. "You still must play the game on the field. However, we now keep a much more keen eye on the scoreboard, with a focus on the vital numbers we believe help us deliver on our goal."

By focusing on the customer and delivering greater return to shareholders, John Deere is moving toward establishing a business as reliable year in and year out as its legendary products.

CHAPTER SEVEN

Put the Brand to Work
(and Protect It at All Costs)

THE BIGGEST COMPETITIVE ADVANTAGE A COMPANY OR BUSI-
ness has over time is its reputation with customers. Employees change and products evolve, but the company that earns
continuing respect and passion for its brand finds distinction
in the marketplace. For John Deere, its reputation for quality and service has grown throughout the company's history
to the point that the brand is stronger in its 168th year of
business than ever before.

"The John Deere brand," said Bob Lane, "is recognized
as a symbol of high-quality products, as well as fair-minded
honorable people who aim to deliver genuine value."

Say tractor, think John Deere. Say green, think John
Deere. And almost anyone who sees the trademark yellow
deer leaping on the green background immediately thinks
John Deere and everything the company stands for. The
brand mark brings to mind John Deere's underlying values,
its reputation, and the level of service the company and its
dealers have maintained, all rolled into one.

It's one of the most recognizable symbols in the world,
representing the John Deere promise that "Nothing Runs

Like a Deere." And it did not happen by accident, because as hard as John Deere has worked through the years on building quality product that performs, the company has worked just as hard at projecting and protecting the symbol that represents it.

THE EARLY IMAGE

Just like John Deere's continuity of employees and leadership, the company has also had a continuity of its brand mark. First appearing in 1876, the leaping deer image has been revised seven times, including most recently in 2000. The first one appeared less than 10 years after founder John Deere and his son and then-company CEO Charles Deere took the legal step of incorporating the agricultural equipment manufacturer as Deere & Company in 1868. The company had operated for 31 years as a partnership or single proprietorship, but had lost on appeal an important trademark case involving its business name John Deere's Moline Plows. Charles Deere sued competitor Swan & Company in 1867 for trademark infringement, noting that the other plow maker was using "Moline" in its advertisements, which looked strikingly similar to Deere's. The company won its case in circuit court in 1969 but later lost on appeal, keeping John Deere from cornering the word "Moline" in trademarks.

At the time, the legal loss was seen as a major setback to John Deere, but Bob Lane notes that it was actually one of several important hinge moments in the company's rich history. The lawsuit prompted the Deere family to rename the company and incorporate it. Work also began developing the corporate identity that has evolved into the popular brand mark that can be seen today all around the world on literally hundreds of thousands of products ranging from tractors and lawn mowers to hats, T-shirts, and license plates.

Recognizing that the company had distinguishing products and characteristics, Charles Deere sought to establish a unique trademark that would serve the company into the future. The result was the leaping deer image, which first appeared publicly in 1876, showing an antlered deer landing after leaping over a log. Included on the image were the words "John Deere" and "Moline, Ill."

The John Deere brand mark evolved six more times before the 1968 version, which included a modified leaping deer and the words "John Deere," and which became the symbol of modern recognition as the company emerged as the world's leading agricultural equipment manufacturer with equally strong trademark recognition.

Naturally there was skepticism, beginning in 1998, when then-chairman and CEO Hans Becherer assigned a cross-discipline team of senior executives to consider updating the John Deere brand mark to more accurately reflect the company's forward progress and global, diversified vision. Not only was the John Deere emblem one of the world's most recognizable, it had evolved into one loved by collectors of company products and licensed goods like the popular green and yellow hats adorned with the logo. Just as when John Deere had replaced its popular two-cylinder tractors in

1960 with its New Generation of Power models, some wondered if the company built on tradition should not just stay the same concerning its brand mark.

But John Deere has endured for more than a century and a half because the company rooted in the ground has never been caught buried in one place. Its leadership and employees have striven to create a modern company based on traditional values, not the other way around. Sure, John Deere's 1968 logo was still recognizable. In fact, in the late 1990s, recognition of John Deere's brand reached an all-time high. The concern was that as the company grew and positioned itself more globally through expansion into areas such as Brazil, China, and India and as the company emerged as a technology leader by using such advances as global positioning satellite systems in its high-end agricultural equipment, the trademark would not accurately reflect John Deere in the twenty-first century as a contemporary corporation.

With the blessing of Becherer and the senior advisory committee, Vice President of Corporate Communication Curtis Linke assembled in spring 1999 more than 200 employees, dealers, customers, students, and representatives of the general public for two dozen, two-and-a-half-hour meetings conducted by a leading branding and design consultancy firm. Research within and by the group revealed that while recognizable, some elements of John Deere's 1968 leaping deer brand mark were not consistent with its current and future direction. The most telling sign: When asked to draw the 1968 trademark from memory, almost 9 out of 10 focus-group participants drew the deer leaping up, not landing, as it was always depicted since first being shown in 1876.

John Deere adopted the eighth logo in 2000 — ironically, this occurred shortly after Lane had taken office, becoming John Deere's eighth chief executive in its long history. The updated mark remained true to its evolving heritage. But because of its sharpened antlers, angles, muscularity, and the fact that for the first time the deer was actually shown leaping upward, the new image better reflected John Deere's transition from being predominantly an agricultural equipment company with primary operations in the United States to its current status as a global organization with interests in a wide range of businesses, from finance to heavy machinery to consumer goods to specialized technology solutions.

The mark depicts what the John Deere brand stands for today: a company proud of its past, preserving and building upon its heritage but simultaneously looking to the horizon for new opportunities. With this modernized leaping deer, John Deere projected an image of moving forward into the new millennium with confidence and power.

"It shows our global strength," Linke said, "and our willingness to embrace new opportunities."

NOTHING RUNS LIKE A DEERE

The origin of John Deere's popular advertising slogan and brand promise to customers did not evolve as carefully or consciously as its leaping deer logo, however. Listed among such timeless slogans as KFC's Finger Lickin' Good and AT&T's Reach Out and Touch Someone, John Deere's Nothing Runs Like a Deere is an all-time great, but it almost

never came to be and originally had nothing to do with tractors or combines.

"Nothing Runs Like a Deere" traces to the early 1970s
when John Deere launched a new line of snowmobiles. The
recreational sport of snowmobiling was taking off in the late
1960s, and more than 100 manufacturers were trying to distinguish themselves and gain share in the fast-growing market. John Deere's entry into the snowmobile business
seemed logical because most sales occurred in the Northern
United States and Canada—areas where Deere already had
strong dealerships in lawn and garden equipment.

Retired John Deere Marketing Director Ralph Hughes
said the company conducted outdoor recreational research
that showed that "the same type of people who were purchasing riding lawn mowers and garden tractors also were
good prospects for snowmobiles."

"They were folks who liked outdoor activities—hunting,
fishing, gardening—and who lived on farms or in rural areas
and small towns," Hughes said.

John Deere entered the competitive snowmobile business in 1971, manufacturing the product at the John Deere
Horicon Works in Horicon, Wisconsin. The product offered
John Deere dealers something besides lawn and garden
equipment to sell in the winter, and the snowmobiles held a
market advantage because they were backed by the proven
John Deere name and its manufacturing legacy dating to
the early 1800s. The equipment was painted green, just like
Deere's trademark agricultural equipment, but the first
snowmobile advertisement ever published contained a
never-before-used company slogan:

Power? John Deere has what you want in your choice of two models, 339 or 436 cc. And we've got something else no other snowmobile offers: Your hometown John Deere dealer with service, parts and experience to keep you on the trail. See him and he'll show you why . . . Nothing Runs Like a Deere.

A John Deere employee for 38 years before retiring in 1992 as the director of advertising for the company's Farm Equipment and Consumer Products division, Hughes was a member of the John Deere committee working with the external advertising agency charged with developing a campaign for the new snowmobile lineup. Bob Wright was a copywriter with the St. Louis, Missouri–based Gardner Agency working on the campaign in 1971. Faced with an impending deadline for a campaign slogan, agency members met into the night, brainstorming and sketching ideas. Wright suggested "Nothing Runs Like a Deere" and jotted it on paper. It got a few good laughs but was ignored due to the assumption that the John Deere team would not like it because it was slightly silly and did not contain the full brand name, "John Deere." The idea was thrown into the trash, Hughes said.

Intrigued by the catchiness, Wright soon revisited the idea and suggested it to the John Deere advertising team. They loved the idea and embraced Nothing Runs Like a Deere as the backbone of the John Deere snowmobile marketing effort, beginning in 1971. The slogan was dropped by the snowmobile group in 1974, yielding to a new theme— Big John—but returned in 1978 and was used until the company ceased snowmobile production in 1982 due to a rapidly contracting industry (the snowmobile industry as a whole, for instance, had shipped 563,000 sleds in 1971, but that number dwindled to 141,000 units in 1982).

Hughes was an advertising manager at John Deere at the time Nothing Runs Like a Deere was first adopted for the snowmobile lineup, and as he progressed in the company, so did use of the slogan throughout the company's Farm Equipment and Consumer Products division. It was soon adopted by the large agricultural division, and today it is used company-wide and has become one of the world's most-recognized advertising slogans.

GREEN MACHINES

John Deere's trademark green products don't have the same carefully planned history as the brand mark. Green was used on products dating back to the early 1880s when the head of Deere's Minneapolis branch complained to Charles Deere that the factory was not doing a good job of finishing implements with "apple green" paint. He suggested to Deere that the "apple green" be restored to its original bright green and darkened as much as possible and yet "remain the same to the eye of the trade." Green was reinforced as John Deere's color when the company bought Waterloo Gasoline Traction Engine Company in 1918, since those products had been painted green with red and yellow trim.

When industrial designer Henry Dreyfuss was hired as a consultant for John Deere's new A and B model tractors in the 1930s and again when he helped design the New Generation of Power lineup in the late 1950s, green was reconsidered as the color-to-be for the company's products. Ultimately, it was decided that green was the best color, and most equipment today is bathed in John Deere's trademark green. Exceptions to this rule include John Deere construction and forestry equipment. In construction equipment, for example, John Deere products are yellow, common to most equipment in the construction segment. The word "Deere" on the side of the product is as large as the "CAT" insignia of its main competitor—Caterpillar. However, the full logo is included somewhere on each piece of equipment to provide the company signature so important to the customer.

This occurred originally because when John Deere had entered the construction business in 1956 Caterpillar and its yellow machinery were as noted in that industry as John Deere's green machinery was in agriculture. Deere entered with yellow products and that has remained. Even the John Deere logo used by the division is yellow on black instead of yellow on green. In recent years, specific John Deere styling, like the styled cabs used on tractors and combines, is increasingly being used on new construction equipment in efforts to better utilize recognizable strengths and traits of the brand.

In forestry equipment, John Deere had also used the construction yellow until making its largest acquisition in company history, buying Timberjack of Finland in 1999 to become the world's leading producer of forestry harvesting equipment. The Timberjack product line uses green and yellow, but not the same hues as the recognized

John Deere colors. Company officials recognize that Timberjack has a strong brand presence in forestry equipment, and for now the name remains, but some believe the colors may be changed to a more traditional John Deere look.

PROMOTE THE BRAND (WITH CARE)

For decades, wearing John Deere hats was popular only on the farm and in rural areas. Then, John Deere experienced growth in the number of collectors who covet everything from antique John Deere tractors and implements to John Deere hats, toys, and Christmas lights. To service the passionate, John Deere built a Collector's Center in downtown Moline.

In the last couple of years, the John Deere brand has experienced an explosion of a broader base. No longer seen on just hats or front-end car tags in rural areas, the image of the yellow deer leaping on the green background has been embraced and worn publicly by such stars as rapper Bow Wow on MTV, actor Ashton Kutcher, and performer Kid Rock. There was George Clooney, who donned it in the movie *The Perfect Storm*. Tennis star Andy Roddick has been seen wearing a John Deere hat. Actor Dennis Quaid sported a John Deere cap on the cover of *Architectural Digest*. Stand outside a boys' prep school when class lets out and count the John Deere trucker-style hats. Ask a metropolitan fashionista about John Deere and get a smile. Rungreen.com, a company specializing in John Deere apparel and memorabilia, experienced a surge in hat sales volume of 800 percent to 1,000 percent in 2003, and children across the country were seen riding battery-powered 4 × 2 John Deere Gator vehicles.

So popular is the John Deere brand that licensing at the company has seen revenue more than double in two years as demand for John Deere boots, flashlights, hats, T-shirts, and hundreds of other items to wear, use, and collect gains in popularity from Moline to Manhattan. A perfect example: When Bold Games and Gabriel Entertainment released an interactive computer game named *John Deere: American Farmer* in 2004, it shot to the top of the charts.

The popularity of John Deere–stamped items dates back to the 1920s when company branch catalogs offered items such as pens, watch fobs, and key chains decorated with the logo. But John Deere began taking its brand to a higher level of exposure at the corporate level beginning in 1995 with the formation of a brand-management group, which has licensed hundreds of products, generating royalties. Sales of John Deere–licensed products increased fivefold from 1995 to 2001 and doubled again by 2004. Items are sold at large, traditional retailers, on specialty web sites, and at John Deere dealerships, which specialize in higher-quality gifts and collectibles like scale-model replicas of popular equipment.

The company licenses the goods for revenue, but the profits are small when compared to what can be derived from $275,000 combines and $175,000 tractors. The biggest reason the company licenses the products is to bring more awareness and brand value to products such as backhoes, tractors, Gators, and lawn mowers.

As product sales grow and as the sale of licensed products increases, the power and recognition of the brand extend far beyond tractors and toys. A Tennessee businessman who owns and operates a farm across the state line in Georgia showed workers his John Deere health insurance card when discussing what plan they might get. Without asking about benefits or available coverage, the workers immediately said they wanted John Deere health insurance, to match the equipment they used every day. The company does not offer health insurance in Georgia, so the men had to go with another company. The point, however, was made. If it's John Deere, it's got to be good for them.

It's a somewhat odd situation, considering that America's farming community is less than 2 percent of the country's population and historically John Deere was viewed as predominantly serving rural America. One assumes, therefore, the company is doing everything possible to put John Deere in front of the public, but that isn't exactly the case. Like any other company working to continually increase its awareness and following, John Deere spends time, effort, and money on marketing and promoting its brand image through advertising, sponsorships, and public relations.

But reflective of the company's deep-rooted, conservative culture, a wary eye has always been cast on promoting too heavily. For many years, in fact, the plan was to focus on building good products, while promoting the brand at the grass-roots level through dealerships and community support. The company has cautiously created a brand that has significant value; some say the brand name alone is worth multiple billions. It can be selective in its public relations efforts, with management choosing when and if to agree to news media interviews, often selecting opportunities with the highly respected news organizations while forgoing other media opportunities that lesser-known companies might use to build a more prominent brand name. The John Deere approach to publicity is also driven by senior leaders who work as a team and do not seek an individual limelight. The public relations (PR) approach is carefully managed to help sustain an image that will not be tarnished by interviews and media plays that do little for the performance of the business.

Beginning in the 1990s, however, even the conservative publicity approach could not slow down a growing awareness of the brand's strength. Conscious steps taken by the company that have resulted in a stronger brand position; these steps had been examined with the same set of core values in mind that had benefited the company throughout its history.

For example, a PGA Tour professional golf tournament had been held in the Quad Cities area for more than 20 years and yet had struggled to maintain a solid title sponsor. Tournament officials decided to approach John Deere. While it was true that the company could gain great public relations from sponsoring such an event, that criterion alone wasn't enough. John Deere crafted a plan that it would become the official golf course equipment supplier to the PGA Tour, recognizing that the designation could launch the golf and turf equipment sales to an all-time high. Event managers within the company also laid out the strong customer and dealer relationship building that could take place during tournament week. Then a plan was conceived on how

Deere could help the tournament increase its contributions to charitable community organizations. In all, the business case was made and the John Deere Classic was born.

Worldwide media coverage has provided John Deere with strong brand exposure, and the company has become known on the PGA Tour as the number-one leader in money raised for charitable causes when judged on a per capita basis for the size of the community.

Another branding opportunity occurred in the 1990s with John Deere's sponsorship in NASCAR's Winston Cup series—the major league of America's stock car racing. However, once again the brand decision was made with a business purpose in mind. The demographics of the NASCAR fan were a near-perfect fit for those who buy John Deere consumer equipment, once again linking a branding opportunity with a strong business purpose. Eventually, though, the cost of racing became a barrier to John Deere's interest in sponsoring an entry in NASCAR. When business results cannot be gained over the cost of a branding opportunity, John Deere's senior leaders are quick to find a better venue for its investment.

A payoff in racing can depend greatly on the success of an individual, and it provides a less certain publicity payoff as it does in a major golf tournament. Consistent with this, John Deere also does not pay money to any specific athlete or celebrity to promote the brand because of the risk in relating too closely to an individual who might become diminished in the eyes of the public. For the same reason, the company does not pay to have products strategically placed in movies or on television as some companies do. The company remains concerned about the impression its core customers maintain concerning the values represented by John Deere.

To exemplify this loyalty to the brand and the company's willingness to aggressively protect it, a story is told about a television show that placed a John Deere cap on the villain—a serial bomber who was terrorizing a city. Within minutes of the character's appearance, dozens of e-mails started arriving at John Deere headquarters from loyal fans of the brand, asking the company to take action against the show. Without offering a full explanation of why the bomber was depicted wearing the John Deere hat, the show agreed to strip the trademark from any reruns after the company quickly communicated the concern.

"We do enjoy a strong base that views us as Americana," said company executive Sam Allen. "We are very conscious that we don't want to do things that offend our core customer. We talk about being defensive so we don't take away what we've built for 168 years."

One reason, it can be assumed, that John Deere's brand is so widely recognized today outside rural areas is the migration of yesterday's "good ol' boy" to suburban areas. Like the old saying goes, You can take the country out of the boy (or girl), but you can't take the boy out of the country. Related to the actual migration is the additional thought that many people yearn for the simpler lifestyle that is represented by a rural setting. In the Southern United States, for example, in 1940 about 7 out of every 10 people lived in rural areas. In the 2000 census, 7 out of every 10 people in the same region lived in urban areas. With them, they have taken an appreciation for rural values, toughness, and pride in machines that work the land. They may never have need for a tractor, but as the passion for John Deere expands beyond the farm, the company is responding to leads in brand placement and licensing that make a positive image to these urban consumers who may want a John Deere lawn tractor or a Gator utility tractor or may need John Deere Landscapes products.

CEO Bob Lane points out that one of the fastest growing product segments for John Deere in the United States is small utility tractors. "Many people have described our tractors to me as their weekend BMWs—a high-quality piece of machinery they can use on their land to escape the pressures of the workweek." These are not large-scale farmers but rather individuals with disposable income who want the best brand they can purchase.

In fact, the company has done extensive research in its consumer equipment lines and determined that many homeowners have purchased John Deere equipment because of the pride they have in owning what is perceived to be the best brand name.

"We are not going to reinvent our brand image," said company executive Sam Allen, "to chase a clothing contract just because for the moment somebody says we are hip. We are going to stay true to who we are. The world is always changing, but we always want to adhere to the same values."

Even as the passion for John Deere grows, trending into

new areas, the same question is always asked corporately when new opportunity arises: What is it going to do to the brand? If the answer is protect, promote, and profit, another project is underway. If even one of the three criteria is lacking, the answer is a swift no. The same test is given to new product initiatives outside licensing.

In the Construction and Forestry Equipment division, John Deere's brand has a different appearance from those of the traditional green products stamped with the yellow logo. Still, the construction and forestry equipment brands are built on the same values of quality, value, and longevity that go along with every John Deere product manufactured since 1837. The same brand-worthiness test is applied to new products and new initiatives in all divisions because employees feel an allegiance to pass along the strengths and tradition of the company.

The company has cultivated its two joint ventures in China, for example. Neither product there currently carries the John Deere name. Why? The product is just now reaching the levels of quality and dependability expected of the world leader in agricultural equipment. The transition has begun now in China to introduce that market to the quality of the brand John Deere.

"John Deere people want to leave something for the next generation," said Construction and Forestry Equipment division president Pierre Leroy, "and they do this by protecting the strength of the John Deere brand. People do not want to mess up the strength of the John Deere brand or what it stands for, so careful consideration is given to all decisions."

Retired chairman and CEO Hans Becherer used to say in employee meetings that it took more than 160 years to create the unique position of the John Deere brand, but the actions of just a few in a short period of time could destroy it overnight. It was a salute to the brand's enduring strength, with a reminder that employees must work to protect it at all costs.

CHAPTER
EIGHT

All Relationships Must Be Win-Win

WHEN BOB LANE TALKS ABOUT INFLUENCES ON HIS LIFE, THE conversation nearly always returns to his family. Raised in Washington, D.C., Lane fondly recalls his parents taking him on Friday nights to the weekly *National Geographic* film series, remembering how it helped him as a young man see the world as a bigger place. When discussing his college choice, he talks of following in the footsteps of his parents and the dreams of his grandfather to Wheaton College, near Chicago.

Lane was a committed rower in high school and Wheaton did not have a crew team, so he decided to swim competitively in college with the belief that Wheaton was the right place. His grandfather, after all, had moved to Chicago and had taken a teaching job there two generations before just so his children could attend the college. His parents had met at Wheaton, as did Bob and his wife, Patty. Today the importance of family remains for Bob and Patty, who live in the quintessential family neighborhood in a smaller community. Even though their three children are grown and living on their own, the Lanes remain very much involved in their lives.

When Bob Lane talks about his three children, it is with pride focused on their humanitarian career choices. Bob and Patty's daughter Kristin also attended Wheaton, and serves as the development director of a homeless shelter in Washington, D.C., while earning her master's degree in public administration. The older son, Peter, graduated from the University of Chicago and Princeton Seminary and teaches in a Philadelphia inner-city public school; Peter's wife, Erin, earned her master's degree in social work in Philadelphia. The youngest of the Lane children, John, graduated from Montana State University and also is a teacher, remaining in Montana where he continues to enjoy his avid love of the outdoors. Bob Lane said, "We are so proud of all four of them."

A BUSINESS IS NOT A FAMILY

At the office, however, Lane makes an important distinction about the term *family* and how it is used by some to define their work colleagues. When he began describing his thoughts, some employees appeared perplexed. Because of its deep-rooted culture and tradition, John Deere is a company that people had in the past often referred to as a family, both externally and internally. We are all, they might say, part of the John Deere family. Or, in tough times, the John Deere family will endure.

Most employees in the majority of companies have compassion for one another, of course, and at John Deere this compassion runs deeper than at many other companies, perhaps because some families have been in the company for generations and because some employees have shared longer-than-average careers side by side with one another. Bonds and appreciation run deep at John Deere. And Bob Lane is known among the workforce to be among the most caring and sincere, remembering thousands of individuals by name and presenting executive speeches in at least three different languages so that employees with different native tongues feel better connected to the message. Like his children, Lane has a decided humanitarian perspective, but he makes it quite clear that he understands that a business is not a family. And for a business to thrive instead of contract in the toughest times, ultimately providing more for families, employees must understand the difference as well.

When speaking to John Deere employees at company facilities around the world, Lane frequently reminds them of this very issue with easy-to-understand illustrations. Lane says, "People talk about the John Deere family, but this is not a family. They are mistaken. If a member of a family has poor behavior, is out of line in their actions, doesn't pull their own weight, or has an unsure level of integrity, they are more than likely still accepted as a member of the family. We all recall an Uncle Harry or some other relative who was odd and perhaps unruly but still welcome at the next holiday. This is not part of the John Deere way. We seek to employ team members, all of whom seek high performance with integrity. Mistakes will be made, but honest, hard effort is required of all. Some people will choose not to be part of the team, and that will be the best decision for them and for John Deere. We must never accept that this is a family that will always accept all who choose to be part of the family, despite their poor performance or low integrity."

John Deere is well-known as a good company to work for, evidenced by the number of years so many employees stay. The company has also been named in recent years as one of the top places to work for workers over 50 by the AARP and has been honored with other workplace awards.

"There is a self-selection by people who choose to aspire to high performance, who choose to work here," Lane said. "They find they are comfortable in this environment where much is expected but where one can be assured that integrity is at the core of our decisions."

The performance management system championed by Bob Lane stresses accountability, a level of promised integrity uncommon in most families. Relationships at John Deere are often long-term and can feel like family, but the definition of the high-performance environment in the making by company leaders is one of teammates. Lane says some people will be uncomfortable and choose to leave. But others like to win as a team, and the company is establishing the culture and reward system to help them do so.

THE BENEFITS OF MUTUAL ADVANTAGE

The business practice of seeking win-win results with all company relationships, including employees, dates back to the earliest days of John Deere's history. Company founder John Deere understood that to be compensated fairly, products must be built with only the highest quality. As the company grew during the 1800s, John Deere established that fairly compensating employees for a day's work was a top priority. The mutual advantage philosophy was articulated by company management into the 1900s as the philosophy became one of John Deere's principles that lived in lore. By the 1960s it was clearly established as a guiding principle of business in the company's first Green Bulletin series published during Bill Hewitt's tenure as chairman. Today, the philosophy continues as a top priority at John Deere, to the point where if you Google "win-win John Deere," the results are plentiful.

How John Deere Develops Win-Win Relationships

- Making customers more satisfied, profitable, and efficient than the customers of competitors, thereby forging lasting relationships.
- Building a dynamic, inclusive business in which diverse employees' contributions are appreciated, respected. and rewarded.
- Delivering substantial shareholder value at all times regardless of the economic, political, and social environments.
- Building mutually profitable and harmonious relationships with business partners—dealers and suppliers among them.
- Contributing to the interests and well-being of the communities where John Deere operates as well as the global community at large.

Bob Lane mentions the win-win phrase in almost every meeting he attends, whether it is with customers, dealers, employees, shareholders, or suppliers. He makes it clear to every person or group that John Deere expects them to work together to find mutual benefit so the relationship will continue successfully. He also reiterated the philosophy when sending out the company's updated Green Bulletin series in 2004, reminding all that no business is sustainable without win-win.

THE LONG-TERM RELATIONSHIP

At John Deere, the philosophy is to approach every relationship as one that could last 75 years or more, whether it is a customer, supplier, or shareholder. It sounds odd at first to use such a large number as a gauge. In this day, not many business relationships last a decade, much less three-quarters of a century. It is not odd at John Deere, considering that many customers, dealers, and employees come from families that have two, three, or sometimes four generations of relationship with the company.

By approaching the relationship as one that could last 75 years or more, John Deere employees must work harder at seeking win-win solutions, because, as Bob Lane notes, if there is not mutual advantage, one of the parties will leave the relationship sooner or later. That's exactly why John Deere launched its initiative to build a business as great as the company's products. Many investor relationships were short-term, simply because investors bought the stock on down cycles, only to trade it on up cycles. It was one area Lane felt strongly that was not being approached with win-win vigor.

"John Deere is a great company to buy products and services from and, for employees, it's a great company to work for, too," Lane said. "But, in comparison, it hasn't been a great investment. Shareholders have not received a consistently good John Deere experience. It must be win-win, for the company and for the shareholder, just like it must be win-win for the dealer, the customer, and the supplier."

THE SYSTEM AT WORK

When John Deere began rebuilding its manufacturing processes around improved supply management in the late 1990s, its commitment to win-win solutions was a leading factor in the company's ability to forge new ways of working with suppliers. At John Deere's Horicon Works in Horicon, Wisconsin, the boom in golf course development around the country, combined with the company's strong products in the market, created stronger-than-anticipated demand for its golf course fairway and green mowers.

Built at Horicon Works, these mowers used parts such as bedknives (precision, multi-edged cutting blades) that were manufactured externally by key suppliers. To effectively deliver the product without stockpiling expensive supply inventory or running the risk of stocking too little, the Deere Horicon management recognized the need to enhance supplier relations and communications in the name of creating just-in-time delivery of product. John Deere began a supplier development program for its Horicon plant, relying on a systemized approach to process reengineering.

Characterized in a detailed case study written by Peter Golden and published in the July 1999 edition of *IIE Solutions*, a publication of the Institute of Industrial Engineers (see www.iienet.org), John Deere Horicon officials approached suppliers such as Fisher Barton, which made the bedknives used in John Deere's mowers, with an offer to analyze and reengineer operations. This would mean that suppliers would have to open the books and processes, sharing sensitive information such as margins and methods with its customer. In manufacturing, the supplier–manufacturer relationship around the world has long been approached with tepid closeness. Each needs the other, but neither wants to divulge too much information in the name of protecting its own profits. When John Deere approached Fisher Barton about deeply analyzing its business relative to bedknive production and delivery, management at the supplier company was skeptical, to say the least.

"I was more than a little concerned," said Dick Wilkey, president of Fisher Barton. "When someone mentions partnership, I get nervous. I know it is going to cost us money."

But John Deere management knew it was vital to improve its supply management processes to profitably manufacture equipment in a cyclical marketplace. Horicon management convinced key suppliers that John Deere expected them to make a profit, and Horicon had no intention of examining records and processes and then siphoning out the lifeblood of suppliers' companies. The solutions to supply management would be win-win so the relationship could grow and prosper for both into the future.

To facilitate John Deere's goal of reducing cycle time production of its products, it had to ensure that products from suppliers would meet its standards for quality, cost effectiveness, and timely delivery. John Deere wanted to be able to call them on a moment's notice and tell them that X amount of additional parts were needed. The deciding factor in preliminary discussions, noted Peter Golden, was that John Deere made it clear that it would not focus just on its own needs but would also analyze the supplier's processes. John Deere, Golden wrote, would treat Fisher Barton "like an internal John Deere department." In return, Fisher Barton's trust would be "compensated with genuine productivity gains and improved financials."

In the end, both John Deere and Fisher Barton reaped significant reward. The supplier's cycle times were reduced dramatically across the board, and John Deere was able to implement a more cost effective build-to-order system at its Horicon facility.

THE HOME DEPOT EXPERIENCE

A longtime strength of John Deere has been its independently-owned dealer base, since the privately owned businesses have been the sales and service agent and community friend to loyal customers for generations. John Deere relies on its dealers to be the community-by-community face of the company, displaying, selling, and servicing its products, and the dealers rely on the company to provide quality products and territorial advantages.

John Deere dealerships, although appearing similar in concept to an automotive franchise, are actually quite different. A high-end combine, for instance, costs $250,000 or more and the machinery is the backbone of larger farming operations with millions of dollars in revenue at stake. When farmers spend that much money on equipment that is so important, the transaction is rarely a cash-and-carry deal. The dealer and the farmer have typically had a relationship for years, and they may have discussed the combine sale for some time. The same is true in the construction business, where dealers must intimately understand a customer's needs for equipment before a sale is made. On the consumer side, Deere dealers also have much stronger relationships with customers because the product line has been considered a premium buy in the homeowner segment.

For its part, John Deere provides the product, the national brand, streamlined financing, and the promise of quality.

But as the landscape of America has changed, so has John Deere's business. The number of dealership owners has decreased, and many dealerships that once sold only agricultural equipment now also sell John Deere's popular consumer lines, primarily including John Deere Gators and riding lawn tractors. In this dealership evolution, many are located closer to suburban areas serving both the rural farmer and the suburban homeowner. But just as the dealerships have undergone change with the shift from rural areas into suburban areas, customers have evolved as well. They want quality products, but often purchase them at big-box retailers like The Home Depot, Wal-Mart, Lowe's, and Sears.

The volume of customers who shop for lawn tractors and similar tools at big-box stores simply can't be matched by the dealership network of smaller stores focused on providing legendary product support for large equipment that must keep running to ensure profitable use for the equipment owner.

John Deere considered a plan to sell parts for its agriculture and lawn products through The Home Depot stores in the mid-1990s in an effort to meet customer demand, but the management feared jeopardizing the win-win proposition with dealers. Testimony to that win-win philosophy is John Deere's position in the walk-behind mower product market. In the consumer products division, John Deere continues producing walk-behind mowers despite selling roughly only 60,000 units per year. The business is small and barely profitable, but John Deere continues it because the dealers want the product to maintain competitive leverage.

When a plan surfaced during Bob Lane's tenure to sell consumer lawn tractors at The Home Depot, company leadership considered it with its typical regard for dealer benefit. A pressing concern was market position in the lawn tractor segment. No one could see John Deere taking a commanding position with a mass channel strategy. Then research unveiled an interesting finding. Consumers preferred to buy their lawn tractors in a mass channel outlet because of the convenience of location and business hours. However, when it came to service, many still wanted to depend on a local dealer to make sure their equipment ran with the precision expected from a purchase of this size.

A what-if plan was under discussion within John Deere. The company's first objective was to obtain mass retail exposure, while strengthening its dealer base at the same time. If that could be accomplished, the Home Depot strategy would work. The concept emerged of aligning dealers with the program by compensating them for all setup of demonstrators at The Home Depot stores and for all deliveries resulting from The Home Depot sales. The dealer would also maintain the premium products not to be sold at The Home Depot, sell products identical to those available through The Home Depot, and have an opportunity for new business through service and future product upselling with customers.

Another John Deere objective was to gain new market share, and ultimately new customers for the company and its dealers, by producing a lower-cost entry-level riding lawn tractor to attract cost-conscious retail buyers. The company's lawn products were considered high in quality, and customer loyalty was high, but John Deere was losing market share in the consumer product arena because its entry-level riding lawn tractor was priced too high (in 1997 an entry-level STX38 retailed for $1,994) for dealers to strongly compete with more accessible, open-at-all-hours retailers. With more volume, a lower price on the entry-level product could be justified. John Deere engineers and product planners were challenged to reduce costs and to find a retail product that would turn heads at The Home Depot stores. The widely held belief was that the product needed a price point below $1,500, instead of one just below $2,000.

With engineers promising to deliver a most price-sensitive product, John Deere executives made the decision in 2002 to sell lawn tractors through The Home Depot nationwide, hoping to take advantage of 22 million customers who trek through 1,400 stores every week. John Deere obtained consumer product exposure like never before almost overnight, but the move was a big shift from business as usual. Management was confident it could retain the win-win relationship with dealers but knew the Home Depot entry would cause initial concern. They were right—John Deere dealers were worried about the move and expressed concern, fear, and even minor outrage that the company was taking what was viewed as a step away from its dealer base to the retail mass market.

So significant was the move when John Deere began selling its L100, entry-level riding lawn tractors at The Home Depot stores in January 2003 that for the first time since the company's founding in 1837, equipment was being sold outside its traditional dealer base. Many John Deere dealers have been partners with the company for many years, some dating back two and three generations. When John Deere told its dealer base it was going to sell product in The Home Depot, many long-time dealers cringed and loudly complained. The criticism, however, quickly died down.

Increased advertising by the large retailer and the relationship many dealers built with consumers created surprising results. The company has stated that more than 100,000 new John Deere customers were created through the sale of the 100 series in The Home Depot just in the first year. A fact that is less known is that sales of lawn tractors also increased in the dealerships, which benefited from the improved product exposure, lower price points, and the avenue to expose consumers to the John Deere way.

Now you can go into any Home Depot on a Sunday night, when traditional John Deere dealerships are closed, and buy a green and yellow riding lawn mower for under $1,500 that also pulls attachments for aerating, seeding, and fertilizing. On Monday, the dealer delivers the product and any attachments and lets the buyer know they want to service the equipment.

John Jenkins, who is president of the worldwide Commercial and Consumer Equipment division of John Deere, explains: "The Home Depot is not in the service business. They are in the mass merchandise business. John Deere dealers are in the service business and are noted for providing world-class service. This program is a model that created a competitive advantage for us. It occurred because we listened to what the customer wanted."

Some industry analysts estimated that the move gained John Deere a market share increase that could be tallied in two digits in a segment where moves of 1 percent annually are significant.

It did not take long for all parties to find these win-win benefits from the Home Depot arrangement. John Deere lawn tractors were an immediate hit at The Home Depot as customers took advantage of the accessibility in both location and hours at the stores. The Home Depot gained the presence of a flagship, consumer-loved brand.

"We learned from the Home Depot experience that our customers will not always come to us," said Jenkins. "We had to go to the customer."

For John Deere dealers, the results were significant as they benefited from greater brand awareness due to heavy Home Depot advertising of the products. They also gained new customers in the process, since dealers located near a Home Depot store can make delivery of the product to the customer. More units are in the marketplace to service, and dealers get the chance to build relationships with new customers who previously may not have known the location and capabilities of their area John Deere consumer product dealer.

"There was a lot of concern," said John Deere dealer Bob Bodensteiner. "We realized it created more opportunity. We sat down and said, 'How can we benefit from this.'"

Bodensteiner said his stores adopted the same selling procedures as the retailer for its consumer products line, selling products at sticker price with no negotiation and not accepting trade-ins. His stores also "moved up a notch" in product offering level and the additional advertising and national awareness helped increase the sales of consumer lawn tractors. So did service revenue, since, no matter where a 100-series lawn tractor is purchased, it is backed by the service of a John Deere dealer.

It's just one example, among many dating back to the company's founding, of how insistence on mutual advantage has allowed John Deere and its many relationships to benefit from a win-win principle.

CHAPTER NINE

Grow on the Strength of Your Roots

THE MOST DIFFICULT AND, AT THE SAME TIME, THE MOST IM-
portant challenge to an already successful company is finding ways to grow that fit well in the corporation and
strengthen, not dilute, the established brand. This challenge
is maximized at John Deere, since its strength is a strong-
hold on a rather unique and isolated industry. Effectively
growing outside agriculture can prove quite difficult and has
at times in the company's history when the method has not
squarely matched the company's main focus.

There has always been an understanding at John Deere
that growth should be carefully considered, dating back to
the company's much-discussed acquisition of the Waterloo
Boy tractor company in 1918 and the acquisition of Lanz of
Germany in the 1950s. Entry into the tractor market and expansion to a more global company both proved to be wise
moves, but some new products, division expansion, and ac-
quisitions have not always worked out as well for John Deere.
Some examples of John Deere's more unique growth at-
tempts are small, like the company's brief entries into the
snowmobile and bicycle businesses.

The company first entered the bicycle business in 1894, at the height of the "great bicycle craze." The first bikes were offered at Deere's Minneapolis branch house, the Deere and Webber Company. The line was produced until 1900 and included the Deere Leader, Deere Roadster, and Moline Special. The Deere Roadster sold for $85 with an option of wood or steel rims.

To build a recreational product line, John Deere made snowmobiles at John Deere Horicon Works in Horicon, Wisconsin, from 1972 to 1984. John Deere's snowmobiles, spanning 21 models over 13 years, were popular and respected for quality, but the industry was too small and the company abruptly quit production, concentrating on equipment that added to the productivity of the user. It was during snowmobile production that John Deere made another attempt at bike sales in an effort to bolster its recreational product line and take advantage of another American "bike craze." The company sold 200,000 bikes between 1972 and 1976, before exiting the business again.

During the farm recession of the 1980s, John Deere suffered severe employee retraction, a deflated stock, and a loss of earnings. In 1986, for instance, the company posted its first annual loss in 53 years ($229 million). Its stock price had fallen from a closing price of $48 per share in 1980 to less than half that value six years later ($22.44). The number of employees working at the company had declined from 59,000 in 1978 to 37,000 in 1986. All along during the down cycle, John Deere continued to invest for growth in the agriculture industry and when it did not occur, the company's troubles were magnified with bloated inventories and costly, unneeded expansion. By the late 1980s and early 1990s, the pressure to grow and diversify in more substantial ways beyond the cyclical agriculture industry hit all-time highs in Moline, and the company began to look far beyond snowmobiles and bicycles.

THE IMPORTANCE OF GROWING IN THE RIGHT DIRECTIONS

In 1991, CEO Hans Becherer separated product lines that did not produce traditional agricultural equipment from John Deere's worldwide Agricultural Equipment division, forming a separate Commercial and Consumer Equipment division. Two years later managed health care and insurance services were separated into divisions so each could be responsible for profit and growth independently. With six separate strategic business units, John Deere had the chance to significantly diversify and grow beyond agriculture for the first time in its history. But with change come lessons to be learned, because the new divisions had to work through finding the difference between good growth and not-so-good growth, and that was to be determined in the field through trial and error.

A longtime John Deere strength was its Credit division, which primarily supported customers and dealers through the financing of equipment. John Deere Credit excelled at knowing and understanding its customer and was successful at blending the principles of lending with years of unique experience in the agriculture industry. On its own and faced with the need to grow in the early 1990s, the Credit division examined opportunities available outside traditional lines of business. "We were asking, Why can't we take what we have done for Deere and do for other companies?" said retired Senior Vice President Mike Orr, previously in charge of the Credit division.

John Deere talked with Coachman, a leader in the recreational vehicle (RV) industry, about offering retail financing to customers buying motor homes. Coachman faced splintered financing options in the RV industry, and John Deere Credit was appealing because it offered one streamlined source dealers could turn to when searching for customer financing. No longer would Coachman dealers face choosing between a multitude of banks and finance companies when shopping around for customers. Just as it had for its own dealers in the agriculture business, John Deere Credit would serve Coachman dealers in the RV business. So promising was the Coachman venture that John Deere Credit also entered into a similar agreement with Outboard Marine Corporation (OMC), financing boats, just as it financed RVs.

But it was not that simple. John Deere Credit entered these new areas of business based on what many considered to be strengths of the company. But what many found was that strengths in the agriculture and construction industry did not translate into strengths in understanding RV and boat loans. "We underestimated the uniqueness of those other industries," Orr said. "They were as unique as the agriculture business."

The biggest problem resulted from John Deere's traditional product quality, which made lending for its own products much easier than lending for others. If John Deere Credit had to collect on a default loan in the agriculture industry, the collateral—a John Deere tractor or combine—was a known and valuable piece of equipment, even used. Additionally, because of the relationship between farmers and John Deere dealers, finding the green equipment was relatively easy. "Ninety-nine percent of the time," Orr said, "we were able to take our own equipment that was used as collateral and resell it through our own internal system. It was equipment that we know and would continue to stand behind."

The story at John Deere Credit was altogether different when it came to RVs and boats. Coachman and OMC made good products, but they were ones that John Deere had little knowledge about. Making matters worse, John Deere Credit did not have a strong enough retail collection system. Finding a boat in Tennessee to repossess, for example, proved almost impossible. Ultimately, the move into expanded retail financing was not a disaster for John Deere Credit. The division made some money and, more importantly, learned valuable lessons and information about its strengths and weaknesses in credit operations, but the outside finance areas were abandoned in the late 1990s.

"We asked ourselves, What is our competitive advantage?" Orr said. "We went back to saying, 'Agriculture is our strength. It is our competitive advantage.'"

The problems John Deere Credit faced when expanding outside its traditional agricultural roots were similar to problems faced by John Deere Health when the division had reached outside its traditional base in the mid-1990s. Long a corporate strength for its ability to manage health care costs for John Deere and other companies in communities where Deere had a strong presence, John Deere Health begged the natural question when growth in the agriculture sector slowed: Can you take the strengths of John Deere Health and extend them into a growth opportunity for the company? The answer was yes, and John Deere Health embarked on a major growth initiative outside its traditional customer circle in John Deere communities.

One of the first lessons learned was that John Deere Health thrived in communities with known and trusted partners where relationships benefited from awareness of the John Deere brand and the company's core values and ways of working. Expansion outside communities and states where John Deere did not have major operations facilities meant dealing with different regulations and different attitudes. John Deere Health experienced a significant loss in 1997, a jolt to the service that had been profitable every year since its inception. In response, John Deere Health retracted, now operating in four states where the company either has a large employee base or had a significant previous relationship that continues working for both parties.

John Deere's acquisition of Homelite in 1994 was also seen as an answer in diversification as the manufacturer of a full line of handheld, outdoor power equipment, including weed trimmers, chain saws, and blowers, seemed a natural complement for the company's business and marketing strengths. John Deere had its own branded higher-end, commercial handheld products, but Homelite would give the company a retail entry to the consumer market. However, even though Homelite was well-known, it was not a benefit to John Deere because its brand power was not nearly as strong.

There was no advantage to John Deere in operating a lesser brand. So what had seemed like a reasonable move in acquiring an existing business actually was a drag on John Deere operations and its brand, resulting in a near disaster from the start. John Deere never made money on Homelite, losing hundreds of millions before it was sold in 2001.

"When we bought Homelite," Bob Lane said, "it was to get into a market we weren't in. But even though we tried mightily, we just could not make it work for us profitably. So, with our renewed emphasis on performance, if our results are not enough to pay the expenses involved, including the cost of capital, we had to quit doing it."

John Deere did not walk away from Homelite or its expansions in John Deere Health and John Deere Credit easily. The company's culture is based on commitment, which, if anything, probably caused it to push too long in wrong directions. The company bases all its relationships on long-term propositions, meaning changes in direction are often met with resistance. The questions are always (1) What will happen to the people? and (2) Can't we make this work? But the realization crystallized with moves away from the center that, while growth will always be vitally important to John Deere, directions of growth are equally as important. As a result, the company focuses growth efforts now in areas that it believes John Deere has or could have a competitive advantage.

By focusing on its purpose to enhance the productivity of its customers, and by seeking opportunities where John Deere's strengths and expertise provide distinct market advantages, the company is able to grow today in ways more complementary of its preeminent status as a global equipment manufacturer. John Deere sticks closer to its core, growing on the strength of its roots and its well-established brand, evolving with its changing customer base.

John Deere's Commercial and Consumer Equipment division, originally called the Lawn and Garden division, began as an outgrowth of serving customers on the farm. John Deere has been for decades the leading provider worldwide of agricultural equipment, adapting with the farming industry as it consolidated into fewer operations requiring larger and more productive equipment. But as North Americans urbanized, their heritage for working the land migrated into suburban areas. Lawns are bigger and more cared for than ever before, and many families have small gardens, some even in metropolitan areas. So while less than 2 percent of the population farms today, an increasing number actually work the land, just in smaller and noncommercial settings.

The Commercial and Consumer Equipment division continues to see opportunities in this trend. In 2003, John Deere introduced a series of all-terrain vehicles, but not with a goal of creating a recreational vehicle. Customer research showed a need to expand the company's already successful utility line with the addition of ATVs geared for work purposes.

At John Deere Credit, such changes have meant growth through new opportunities within an existing and growing customer base. The division now provides its agricultural customers more than equipment loans, serving as more of a full-service financing option as farmers look to streamline more aspects of operations. Financing crops is certainly more complex than financing a tractor, but John Deere Credit has generations of experience with farmers, understands traits and tendencies, and is providing John Deere customers in more than a dozen countries with multiple financing services. And as John Deere expands its consumer product offerings and base, John Deere Credit has thousands of more natural opportunities than what was offered in boats and RVs.

SERVING THOSE WHO WORK THE LAND

Defining the land and those who work it is the primary basis for considering new opportunities. Indeed, there is a new, trendy John Deere bike on the market, but it is a licensed product and not manufactured by the company. Items such as the bike help create brand awareness. Efforts to grow the business are more substantial.

John Deere's Golf and Turf group produces a full array of golf course management products ranging from top-of-the-line fairway, rough, and greens mowers to bunker rakes, aerators, and implements designed specifically to remove debris from the course. John Deere's sponsorship of a PGA

Tour event in 1997 made it the official golf course equipment supplier to the tour's Tournament Players Club (TPC) courses around the country and signaled the company's establishment as a premier provider of golf course equipment and solutions. Deere is known now as an innovator in the industry, recently introducing a hybrid greens mower that runs on electricity when noise is an issue (which it often is on the golf course) and on gasoline after hours. More importantly, the use of sophisticated electronics on the machine eliminated more than 100 locations on past models where hydraulic fluid could have leaked—a leading irritant to golf course superintendents who cannot afford to have equipment damage well-manicured greens. The product line was an instant hit with those responsible for golf course management.

Often growth comes in evolutionary ways, points out company executive Sam Allen. "We want to grow consistent with our values and we want it to be a steady progression. In turf care equipment, for instance, first we made high-care lawn equipment and now we have evolved to also make sophisticated golf course maintenance equipment taking advantage of lessons learned in engineering and product design."

Many growth opportunities for John Deere exist with current customers or customers in the same demographic as its current customers in areas outside of heavy equipment, because, while three-fourths of the company's revenues come from equipment sales, equipment purchases account for only a few cents of every dollar spent on the average farm site, work site, or home site. Since John Deere is a trusted name, new opportunities are many. A prime example is

John Deere Landscapes, which generated more than $400 million in revenue in one year after becoming a full-fledged company operation.

The landscape division began in 2001 when the company purchased existing landscape distributor McGinnis Farms. It quickly expanded, purchasing other companies that specialized in such areas as irrigation supply, to become the nation's largest wholesale distributor, serving more than 200 branches in 39 states and Ontario, Canada. Acting as the wholesaler, John Deere Landscapes creates personal relationships with landscapers and contractors, providing full lines of landscape and irrigation supplies, including ornamental nursery stock and landscape lighting. The division is profitable, growing, and creating multiple cross-selling opportunities for John Deere in equipment, finance, service, and parts. John Deere Credit, for example, allows its partner landscapers to arrange for consumer loans to get their work done.

"John Deere Landscapes," Deere CEO Bob Lane said, "illustrates how we can extend our competencies to provide more services for customers and deliver value to customers in new ways and ones that provide profitable growth."

John Deere's biggest existing divisions are growing as well by sticking close to the plan of serving customers who work the land. In the construction equipment industry, Caterpillar is the preeminent brand and the positioning is somewhat different for John Deere. But the company is finding growth in construction equipment by delivering John Deere's quality and value proposition to customers. The company has purposefully consolidated to just more than 50 dealer–owners from a high of 400, streamlining its service and support end of the construction and forestry equipment business. Through consolidation, the company maintained its best and strongest dealers and is now able to implement such standards as a signature process, designed to help the dealers know more about their customers.

The Construction and Forestry Equipment (C & F) division is also subtly integrating some of the best qualities of its Agricultural Equipment division into construction equipment to leverage strengths from other lines and provide a full John Deere experience. One reason that Deere construction and forestry equipment is yellow, not green, is because the company initially wanted to distance C & F from Agricultural. However, today design and product development in one line can benefit another.

And just as the Agricultural Equipment division has changed the way farmers work, the Construction division is working to change the way contractors work. One prototype on Deere's drawing board is the Bison, an alternative to grading with traditional dozers that leave tracks on sites and are not as fast. The Bison incorporates the same recognizable cab used on John Deere harvesters and top-of-the-line tractors. Another product on the drawing board is a "swing steer backhoe," which would allow operators much greater rotating flexibility on work sites.

Whether Deere builds its prototype construction products remains to be seen, but division president Pierre Leroy says the developments show how the company is seeking to meet the demands of its contractor customers and deliver a value promise of productivity, more uptime, and a lower daily operating cost.

In agriculture, farming may be contracting in North America in terms of the number of farmers working the land, but John Deere's growth opportunities are far from limited globally as the need for more food production rapidly increases. The driving factor of food consumption is wealth, since the amount of money people have directly correlates to how much they eat and what types of foods they eat. A wealthier populace, for instance, consumes far more pork than a poor populace. If it takes five pounds of grain to grow one pound of pork, the consumption of grain dramatically increases as emerging economies like Brazil and China grow.

"The agriculture business is straightforward," said David Everitt, president of the agriculture division for Europe, Africa, the Middle East, and South America. "People have to eat and they are going to eat more. We have to position ourselves where the growth is going to occur."

Brazil is the hottest market in agriculture and John Deere is well-positioned there for growth. The company entered Brazil in 1979 through a partnership and began manufacturing products in its own plant and under its own trade name in 1999. In 2004, John Deere announced construction of a new 500-employee tractor plant in Montenegro, Brazil, in efforts to capture market share. In 1966, for instance, combine industry sales in Brazil totaled just three machines. Today, combine sales are almost 7,000, and that's only the beginning since literally thousands of acres across the country's plains are being moved into farm production each year.

Food demands are increasing in John Deere's largest markets as well, including North America and Europe, and growth is also forecast to meet future nonfood uses of grain like ethanol and biodiesel fuel production. The availability of usable land, and more importantly, the availability of water, will be significant factors, but John Deere is forecasting growth in the global agriculture market over the next quarter of a century and is preparing to maintain its position as the world leader in agricultural equipment.

Additionally, the company is expanding its relationship with agricultural producers by providing solutions outside of horsepower-based equipment. By providing high-tech solutions such as AutoTrac precision steering in tractors and combines, the company is actually helping farmers solve human resources issues since previously finding equipment operators to drive close to an exact line in the field proved difficult. And, by sharing environmental information with farmers and assisting them with credit solutions, the company is playing a larger role in production.

"Our DNA says we must look like a tractor or a combine to the farmer," John Deere division president H.J. Markley said. "But the product is only part of it. We are going back and trying to understand our customer's business beyond the field."

Maintaining customer affordability as John Deere races to offer more productivity, innovation, and operating comfort in its equipment will always be a challenge. The agricultural equipment industry learned a painful lesson in the 1980s when the market determined that it would not or could not pay for new equipment during the recession. Yet the demands for improvements and innovation never go away.

In recent years, John Deere customers have benefited from lower interest rates, which absorbed equipment price increases. The annual payment on an 8000 Series John Deere tractor in 1997, for example, was $18,624. Payment on a new 8000 Series tractor in 2003 was just $19,221, despite product price increases totaling 16 percent over that period of time. Lower interest rates resulted in the customer paying just 3 percent more for the same, albeit improved product.

External pricing factors, like steel prices, can't be controlled, but when it comes to development, John Deere works to deliver higher productivity, making costly equipment more valuable investments. The result is that future growth in high-end agricultural equipment will increasingly be driven by innovation that lowers farm overhead in other areas. An operatorless combine that harvests with precision, summoning an operatorless truck when its grain bin nears capacity, and unloads without stopping may seem like something only a farmer would dream.

But John Deere has already produced an advanced concept, driverless tractor that traverses fields with pinpoint accuracy due to its precision Global Positioning System (GPS) technology. For the company that has thrived on having the right products at the right time, making it a consumer reality and creating another opportunity for growth may not be too many years into the future.

CHAPTER
TEN

Performance That Endures

FEW WILL DEBATE THAT JOHN DEERE IS A GREAT COMPANY. Despite depressions, recessions, and cyclical business, it has endured, serving customers for 17 decades by providing those who work the land with products and services that typically make their jobs and lives easier or more enjoyable, and sometimes both. But finding its secret to success is not as easy as identifying one area like exemplary product or focusing on the customer who has made the biggest single difference. The qualities that make John Deere a leading global company date back to its very beginning and have accumulated over time, layering over one another like rings of a tree trunk. The new has built on strengths of the old, resulting in a homogeneous structure that stands taller in its 168th year of business than ever before in its history.

In the beginning, it was mostly about productivity. Blacksmith John Deere talked and listened to farmers, determining needs and seeking solutions. His first product, the self-scouring plow, was utility in the highest degree, but at the time it was exactly what farmers in the Midwest needed to get their jobs in the fields done more effectively and in less time. Dozens of other, much larger companies were making plows in America in the early- and mid-1800s, and another Midwesterner (John Lane, distant cousin of Bob Lane) was even experimenting with a steel plow of his own invention. However, John Deere's personal commitment to products and installation of values into his fledgling company created a foundation based on standards that allowed his enterprise to grow and continue serving customers.

When John Deere's son, Charles, took over upon the founder's retirement, transforming the company during the late 1800s from a smaller, family-style operation into a more national, multimillion dollar corporation, the original core values of business remained. The company's product breadth spread far beyond its original steel plow, but it was still all about productivity, strengthened by the founding tenets of quality, innovation, integrity, and commitment. The business, however, became a focus parallel to the products as the company expanded beyond its Mississippi River base with the creation of decentralized branch houses, which partnered with Deere & Company to sell products from Kansas City to San Francisco.

When the growing implement manufacturer purchased the Waterloo Boy tractor company in 1918, it made an acquisition that dramatically altered its corporate course. As a tractor manufacturer, John Deere's business rapidly expanded, reaching thousands of new customers and earning lasting respect among many for displaying an ongoing commitment to product quality, reliability, and service. It was still about productivity, but the company emerged from the masses of other agricultural equipment manufacturers at the time as a leader due to strength from its compounded foundation anchored by the values of founder John Deere.

By the time the company reached the mid-1900s, its founding family was still involved in corporate leadership, and the legacy of building quality products and always standing behind them was well-established in plants, at dealerships, and in executive offices. But just as the company had evolved from its founding with such changes as increased emphasis on the business and the addition of tractor manufacturing, another shift paving the company's path to success would occur in the late 1950s and early 1960s. It would be the most decisive, separating John Deere from its competitors and fueling the beginning of a contemporary era of agriculture where the passion and desire of farmers were recognized and served along with their need for utility.

THE IMPORTANCE OF PRIDE
AND PRODUCTIVITY

The American farm in 1960, of course, was typically a place of simplicity, isolated from the tastes, movements, and progressions of trending urban areas due to limitations in communication and resources. Many rural areas still lacked electricity, telephone connections were party lines where neighbors could answer one another's phone calls, television meant rabbit ears and one fuzzy station, and children were allowed to miss school to work the fields during harvest. Upscale shopping was confined to only the largest cities and unpaved roads were the rule, not the exception.

The decision, then, for Bill Hewitt and John Deere to introduce striking design and bold new power in tractors to the agricultural community in 1960 was pioneering in its own right. By uniquely blending urban style and comfort with rural power in its New Generation of Power tractors, the company became the first on a large scale to add pride to productivity for farmers. And how it was revealed to the world was as important, perhaps, as the change itself. A big, green, diamond studded John Deere tractor was unveiled next to the jewelry counter inside the Neiman Marcus department store! It was so utterly farfetched for the times, it was outrageously successful.

For John Deere, it changed everything. The company's reputation with consumers expanded far beyond quality and reliability. As a result, John Deere quickly became the world leader in agricultural equipment. At the same time, a move was made to the new headquarters facility that reflected John Deere's broad, contemporary mission. The building reinforced the company's commitment to its small, Midwest home. It also revealed a vision that extended far beyond the banks of the Mississippi River.

But even as John Deere surged to the top and continued to grow, through more products and services and global expansion, the company maintained its core values, allowing new directions to be foundation additive, not altering. The company and its dealer network continued to focus on customer relationships and service. Continuity of leadership and a pass-along method of management remained. Company employees continued to foster a culture that rewarded doing business the right way. Productivity still mattered, maybe more than before. But pride mattered as well, particularly with the customer.

As a result, the company and its products emerged during the second half of the twentieth century as iconic symbols of quality and value. The brand stood for everything great about the products, and the products stood for everything great about the brand. Or, as one longtime customer explained, by delivering pride and productivity, John Deere equipment became the farmer's BMW, coveted as the ultimate agricultural machines.

The company's business, however, did not follow the same, steadily rising arc charted by the products and the brand, due to the cyclicality of the equipment business. Some years, the business was great, while other years, the business was terrible. The products continually improved, the brand continually strengthened, and core values remained, but the company typically faced either feast or famine in bottom line results.

The 1970s, for instance, were great. Hiring boomed, products sold in record numbers, and profits were high. The 1980s, though, were awful. Contraction was so painful it took a fighting spirit just to survive. The 1990s were both rewarding and stressful, as business restructuring benefited John Deere in mid-decade growth, but recessionary pain resurfaced again by 1998. Along the way, investors bought the stock at down cycles and sold it in up cycles, waiting for better buying opportunities. Employees learned to enjoy the good times and brace for the bad, accepting that business turbulence came with the territory of equipment manufacturing.

BUILDING A BUSINESS AS GREAT AS THE PRODUCTS

When Bob Lane became chairman and CEO in 2000, John Deere was still mired in a difficult industry down cycle that would get worse with the bursting of the American economic bubble and the tragic events of September 11, 2001. As always, the products were good. In fact, they were better than ever before. The commitment was the same, and the brand was experiencing unprecedented exposure. But the business was a headache. Lane's resolution was that by giving the shareholder the same attention that the company had given to its products and customers for so many years, John Deere would take another step forward in its evolving corporate history, building a sustainable great business.

"We had established we can distinctively serve customers," Lane said. "We can do better, and do it in more places, and we will. We had established we have great products. They can be better and we know how to make them better. But we did not have a great business."

The battle to build a sustainable great business was not a shift away from previous qualities that had helped John Deere become a leading global company. Instead, it was another added layer to the foundation that makes John Deere a great company. Core values—*how* business is conducted—continue as the basis for the lean business model. And emphasis on the shareholder means that John Deere must continue to perform for customers and employees to deliver returns year after year. It's just a matter of adding pride and productivity to the business element of the John Deere way.

"Our job is to run a great business under all market conditions," Lane said. "It is simply taking the John Deere legacy to the next level."

THE FUTURE OF GREEN

As John Deere progresses into the home stretch of its second century of business, its biggest challenge will be maintaining the culture that understands the company's pass-along legacy of values and the tradition of building on its strengths. Because so little hiring occurred at John Deere in the 1980s and because more than 30 percent of its employees have 20 years or more with the company, a third of its white collar workforce will become eligible for retirement in this decade.

Those who join the company from either the college campus or another setting will discover that their qualifications, of course, must include a commitment to the ethics and business morals that have served the company since 1837. And they must want to excel in the unique corporate world that is John Deere. "The secret ingredient is passion," said Sam Allen. "You can get smart, highly trained people, but to get them passionate . . . that's something you don't get easily."

The John Deere Promise

At John Deere, we remain true to our core values of quality, innovation, integrity and commitment. From the first polished-steel plow in 1837 to the cutting edge innovations of today, people trust us to deliver the best that is within us. This is not only our legacy, it is our purpose—to create and sustain an exceptional experience of genuine value for customers, employees and shareholders.

We have a passion for being the leading performance company everywhere we do business. Performance drives us as an organization. We set clear goals and take responsibility for reaching them as individuals and as members of the John Deere team. In return, we share in the rewards created by our actions.

At John Deere, success is not just for the moment, but also for the long run. We deliver performance that endures.

Ultimately, they must learn and understand that the John Deere secret to success is its legacy, built in layers, year after year and generation after generation. It is how the company from Moline, Illinois, became a world leader, delivering performance that endures through pride, productivity, and a great business.

John Deere Leadership

John Deere, 1837–1859

The founder invented the steel walking plow, which transformed farming in the Midwest due to its ability to cut through sticky soil. He instilled four core values, including quality, innovation, integrity, and commitment, that remain with the company today.

Charles Deere, 1859–1907

John Deere's son took over the company at the age of 21, running it for 49 years. During his tenure, annual sales increased from less than $200,000 to more than $3 million. At his death in 1907, the company was at least as strong as any others in the agricultural manufacturing industry.

William Butterworth, 1907–1928

Married to Katherine Deere, the daughter of Charles Deere, Butterworth took charge of Deere & Company as chief executive officer when his father-in-law passed away in 1907. Butterworth was a lawyer with conservative views on business and stressed loyalty, trust, and service to company employees. He presided over the consolidation of the company into what is its modern form. He retired from Deere in 1928 to head the U.S. Chamber of Commerce.

Charles Deere Wiman, 1928–1955

A great-grandson of company founder John Deere, Charles Deere Wiman became the fourth Deere family member to run the company in taking over for William Butterworth. Under his leadership the size of the company increased from $64 million to $340 million as he emphasized product design, efficient production, and engineering excellence.

William A. Hewitt, 1955–1982

The company's fifth chief executive officer, the son-in-law of his predecessor, Charles Deere Wiman, was the last representative of the Deere family to run the company. He had a taste for design and a global vision and raised the company's sights far beyond its Midwestern roots. Hewitt oversaw the design and completion of John Deere's timeless world headquarters facility in Moline and was behind the successful Deere Day in Dallas in 1960. Also under Hewitt's tenure, John Deere became the world's leading manufacturer of farm equipment.

Robert A. Hanson, 1982–1989

Hanson was the first CEO to be unconnected with the Deere family. He led the company to an increase of annual sales from $4.6 billion to $7.2 billion despite the fact that the agricultural industry was in a significant downturn during his tenure.

Hans W. Becherer, 1989–2000

Responsible for launching John Deere's Genuine Value program, Becherer led the company to diversify through global expansion and to strengthen internal operations by separating them into divisions. During Becherer's term John Deere sales increased from $7.2 billion annually to $13.8 billion and earnings topped $1 billion for the first time.

Robert W. Lane, 2000–Present

Lane became John Deere's eighth CEO following a career at the company that included positions as president, chief financial officer, and managing director of operations in Europe, South Africa, and Asia. Lane introduced the "Building a Business as Great as Our Products" concept to John Deere and is noted for leading the company when it delivered unprecedented increases in shareholder value.

B

Key Dates in
John Deere History

1837 John Deere fashions a polished-steel plow that lets pioneer farmers cut clean furrows through sticky Midwest prairie soil.

1838 John Deere, blacksmith, evolves into John Deere, manufacturer. Later he remembers building 10 plows in 1839, 75 in 1841, and 100 in 1842.

1843 Deere and Leonard Andrus become "co-partners in the art and trade of blacksmithing, plow-making and all things thereto . . ."

1848 The growing plow business moves to Moline, Illinois, 75 miles southwest of Grand Detour. Moline offers water power and transportation advantages. Deere chooses a new partner, Robert N. Tate, who moves to Moline and raises the rafters on their three-story blacksmith shop by July 28.

1852   Deere buys out his partners. For the next 16 years, the company is known variously as John Deere, John Deere & Company, Deere & Company, and Moline Plow Manufactory.

1859   Charles Deere takes over at age 21 and runs the company for 49 years.

1867   Charles Deere sues Candee, Swan & Co., a competitor, for trademark infringement. The case has precedent-setting implications for trademark law. Could Deere preempt the word "Moline," which it has been using in its advertising, so that no similar product could incorporate it? The ultimate answer is no. The Walking Cultivator is patented in August 1867. Although farmers might prefer riding, the lower cost of this unit makes it sell even though the farmer has to walk in soft ground while straddling a row of corn.

1868   After 31 years as a partnership or single proprietorship, the concern is incorporated under the name Deere & Company. There are four shareholders at first, six within a year. Charles and John Deere control 65 percent of the stock.

1869   Charles Deere and Alvah Mansur establish the first branch house, Deere, Mansur & Co., in Kansas City. A semi-independent distributor of Deere products within a certain geographic area, it is the forerunner of the company's current farm and industrial-equipment sales branches and sales regions.

1877 Deere & Mansur Company is formed in Moline to manufacture corn planters. A separate organization from the similarly named Kansas City branch, it will become part of Deere & Company in 1909.

1886 John Deere dies in Moline at 82.

1907 Charles Deere dies. William Butterworth, his son-in-law, becomes CEO. The company establishes a noncontributory pension plan for employees with 20 or more years of service who have passed age 65.

1912 The modern Deere & Company emerges. It consists of 11 manufacturing entities in the United States and 1 in Canada, and 25 sales organizations—20 in the United States, including an export department, and 5 in Canada. The company also operates a sawmill and owns 41,731 acres of timberland in Arkansas and Louisiana. Harvester Works is built in East Moline.

1918 Deere buys the maker of Waterloo Boy tractors. The tractor will become its basic product. Though 5,634 Waterloo Boys are sold this year, Ford Motor Company sells 34,167 Fordson tractors.

1931 A $1.2 million embezzlement at People's Savings Bank (Deere's Bank) in Moline, Illinois, threatens closure and loss of employee savings. The company writes a check to cover the loss. The bank survives.

1934 Despite the Great Depression, the company emphasizes product development. The Model A tractor enters production. A similar but smaller Model B follows in 1935. They become the most popular tractors in the company's history, remaining in the product line until 1952.

1938 Industrial designer Henry Dreyfuss, working with Deere engineers, streamlines the A and B tractors. Henceforth, concern for attractive design joins traditional utilitarian values as hallmarks of John Deere products.

1955 William A. Hewitt is elected president and later CEO following the death of Charles Deere Wiman, his father-in-law. He will direct the company for the next 27 years, the last representative of the Deere family to do so.

1956 The firm steps toward becoming a multinational manufacturer. The company decides to build a small-tractor assembly plant in Mexico and buys a majority interest in a German tractor and harvester maker with a small presence in Spain. In the next few years, Deere will move into France, Argentina, and South Africa.

1960 Four New Generation of Power tractor models steal the show at Deere Day in Dallas. Some 6,000 attend the sales meeting, including all U.S. and Canadian dealers.

1963 John Deere surpasses IH to become the world's largest producer and seller of farm and industrial tractors and equipment. The company ventures into the consumer market, deciding to produce and sell lawn and garden tractors plus some attachments such as lawn mowers and snow blowers.

1964 The Deere & Company Administrative Center opens. Designed by Eero Saarinen, it will win many architectural awards. Goals of the company and the principles behind its basic policies and procedures are outlined in the Green Bulletins.

1970 Deere reorganizes its management structure to reflect growing diversification. Three operating divisions emerge: Farm Equipment and Consumer Products, United States and Canada; Farm Equipment and Consumer Products, overseas; and Industrial Equipment, which has worldwide responsibilities.

1971 Nothing Runs Like a Deere advertises snowmobiles, a new product of the John Deere Horicon Works. The slogan lasts far longer than the snowmobile line, which is sold in 1984.

1982 Robert A. Hanson succeeds retiring Chairman William A. Hewitt.

1990 Hans W. Becherer, president since 1987 and CEO since 1989, is elected chairman upon the retirement of Robert Hanson.

1993 New 5000, 6000, and 7000 Series tractors drive up market shares in North America and Europe. Among 20 contenders in Germany, Deere moves from third to first place in tractor sales. Lawn-and-garden-equipment sales top $1 billion for the first time.

2000 Hans Becherer reaches retirement, and Robert W. Lane is elected CEO. Deere acquires Timberjack, a world-leading producer of forestry equipment. A new tractor plant is opened near Pune, India. Credit offices are established in Argentina and Brazil. Deere is granted a banking license in Luxembourg, allowing John Deere Credit ability to finance equipment throughout Europe.

2003 Through agreement with The Home Depot, riding mowers are sold in the mass channel for the first time in company history.

John Deere Green Bulletins

(Updated and reissued by Robert W. Lane, August 2004;
this is an outline of the principles listed
in the complete, updated Green Bulletin series.)

No. 1—Vision Statement

Our vision, our aspiration, is to distinctively serve customers—those linked to the land—with a business as great
as our products. Such a business consistently delivers greater
value to all who have an interest in our success. Achieving
our vision requires exceptional operating performance, disciplined Shareholder Value Added (SVA) growth and
aligned, high-performance teamwork.

No. 2—Core Values

Our reputation is based on the four core values embodied
by our founder: integrity, quality, innovation and commit-

ment. The statement "I will not put my name on a product that does not have in it the best that is in me," attributed to John Deere himself, captures the spirit of these values. It guides us in our pursuit of exceptional performance.

No. 3—Commitment to Employees

Our successful history is due in large part to the dedication to excellence by committed employees, beginning with John Deere himself. We strive to provide a rich employment experience for all, with respect for individual viewpoints. By following consistent principles we can fairly and effectively meet individual employees' high expectations.

No. 4—Commitment to Customers

John Deere customers expect the best return on their investment in terms of product features, quality, availability and price. Our long record of success in the marketplace is based on our fundamental commitment to meeting customers' high expectations in every transaction. This has allowed us to develop legendary relationships with loyal customers that lead to genuine value for all John Deere customers, employees and shareholders.

No. 5—Commitment to Shareholders

John Deere started our company by creating a quality product that met or surpassed basic customer needs. Over time, he earned the fruits of his labor and his investment grew with the company's success. Today, our shareholders, the people who invest their money in Deere, own the company. Much like John Deere himself, today's owners expect to receive long-term financial gains in return for their investment.

No. 6—Global Business and Diversity

John Deere pursues sustainable, profitable business opportunities around the globe by applying our exceptional competencies and capabilities in new situations. Guided by our objectives for enterprise profitability and growth, we seek out customers whose needs we understand and can serve exceptionally well.

No. 7—The Way We Work Together

As a diversified company, we compete in many markets around the world. This challenges us to organize and manage the company in a way that balances each unit's ability to optimize its potential with larger unit, division or corporate goals for exceptional performance.

No. 8—Business Ethics and Compliance

We choose to operate Deere & Company by a standard of business ethics that is rooted in the company's core values of integrity, quality, commitment and innovation. These values form a consistent framework to guide our decisions and actions. Always doing our best to operate within this framework, we have earned a preeminent reputation for ethical business conduct that is trusted around the world. It is a competitive business advantage that all employees are responsible for preserving and enhancing.

No. 9—Environment, Health and Safety

The John Deere organization places great value on environmental protection and human safety. We are highly regarded for our policies and practices, which advocate the well being of the Earth and its citizens. As a global manufacturer, we strive to conduct our business in a manner that safeguards our employees, customers, community neighbors, suppliers, and environment.

No. 10—Public Responsibility

Our primary goal as a global, publicly-owned company is to provide goods and services that society wants and needs, determined by their value in the marketplace, in a way that delivers expected financial returns for our owners. Sustained exceptional business performance is how we both carry out that role and measure our success in doing so. The company also demonstrates its commitment to the betterment of society through products and services that deliver value for our customers, ultimately leading to improvement of the human condition.

No. 11—Performance That Endures

John Deere employees thrive on creating exceptional John Deere experiences for our customers, shareholders, and others who are affected by, or influence the company's success. *How* we as employees carry out our individual responsibilities is as important as the success we achieve. John Deere employees know that the "means" is every bit as important as the "end." Doing the right things at the right time is how we create a sustainable business that is admired around the world.

No. 12—The John Deere Brand

Throughout our history, generations of employees performing their work with care and passion on behalf of customers have made the John Deere brand universally accepted as a mark of value. Each John Deere employee has a responsibility to protect the value of the John Deere brand by acting in accordance with the values it has come to represent—integrity, quality, commitment, and innovation.

APPENDIX
D

John Deere Strategy

WE ASPIRE TO DISTINCTIVELY SERVE CUSTOMERS—THOSE linked to the land—through a great business, a business as great as our products. To achieve this aspiration, our strategy is:

- Exceptional operating performance
- Disciplined SVA growth
- Aligned high-performance teamwork

Exceptional operating performance is both earning our customers' business with highly valued offerings and relentlessly improving global operations, highlighted by a focus on asset efficiency.

We work to be first—to earn sustained preeminence in the eyes of our customers, those linked to the land. As a result, we reach for leading or preeminent market positions with lifestyle consumers who enjoy the land; contractors and landscapers who work the land; and foresters and agricultural producers around the globe who harvest the land.

Customers determine when our products are great. A great business serves their needs. In a great business, all product offerings and supporting activities are of high quality and deliver exceptional operating return on operating assets for equipment operations and a 15 percent return on equity for nontransfer priced financial services. The result is sustained shareholder value added (SVA).

Disciplined SVA growth is investing the cash generated from exceptional operating performance in energized growth initiatives that enhance SVA, in addition to directly returning it to our investors.

We drive to grow SVA through innovation, invention, and accelerated customer focus. We grow by expanding our existing businesses, delivering the pride and profit of advanced mobile productivity. In addition, we pursue logical extensions such as tracing food origins, enriching landscape and forestry resources, harnessing water, financing production agriculture, and harvesting wind and other rural energy.

Customer needs launch our SVA growth initiatives. We seek customers on farm sites, work sites, home sites, and recreational sites across the world whose needs we understand and can serve exceptionally well. Using a disciplined investment process and maintaining our strong balance sheet, we invest where we can leverage our reputation, our culture, and our extraordinary ability to integrate competencies and technologies derived from our global business.

Aligned high-performance teamwork is linking employee, unit, and divisional goals and compensation to global enterprise objectives for exceptional operating performance and disciplined SVA growth.

We aim high to win, celebrating successes and enthusiastically pursuing new levels of enterprise performance. Working as a team—aligned across divisions worldwide and with dealers, suppliers, and partners—creates a unique, hard-to-copy competitive advantage for John Deere. Optimizing a winning enterprise performance, and sustaining it, multiplies opportunities and rewards for all.

Customers' focus drives high-performance teamwork. John Deere employees working together make us a leading performance company everywhere we do business. This fully aligned global organization, supported by a robust employee performance management and development process, also creates exciting opportunities for advancement, fulfillment, and reward. Our leaders at all levels are recognized not only for their ability to deliver results, but also for how they deliver them. Employees of diverse backgrounds and geographies sustain our core values of integrity, commitment, and innovation.

John Deere's Business

JOHN DEERE IS ORGANIZED INTO FOUR MANUFACTURING segments, including Agricultural Equipment, Commercial and Consumer Equipment, Construction and Forestry Equipment, and John Deere Power Systems, with the first three normally providing more than 85 percent of total company revenues. Products and services in the equipment segments are marketed primarily through independent John Deere retail dealers or major retail outlets. The company also provides financial solutions to customers and dealers with John Deere Credit and serves four states through John Deere Health. John Deere net sales and revenues totaled almost $20 billion in 2004, as worldwide equipment sales increased 14 percent.

Agricultural Equipment—John Deere has been the global leader in agricultural equipment since 1963. This division manufactures and distributes a full line of farm equipment and service parts, including tractors; combine, cotton, and sugarcane harvesters; tillage, seeding, and soil preparation machinery; sprayers; hay and forage equipment; material handling equipment; and integrated agricultural management systems technology.

Major customers for the Agricultural Equipment division include large and small farmers from around the world. Leading products in John Deere's largest division include the 60 Series STS combines, which can weigh more than 32,000 pounds and deliver 375 horsepower. Included in the agricultural equipment line are the popular tractors, ranging in size from entry-level 18-horsepower compact utility units to the 500-horsepower, four-wheel-drive 9020 Series designed for heavy-duty field work and featuring FieldVision lighting for nighttime vision.

John Deere's Agricultural Equipment division generated more than $9.7 billion in sales worldwide in 2004.

Commercial and Consumer Equipment—Serving homeowners, commercial mowing and grounds care operators, golf course maintenance operations, and even farmers and contractors, John Deere's Commercial and Consumer Equipment division became a separate corporate entity in 1991.

John Deere first manufactured lawn mowers in 1963 but today provides full-scale lawn and ground care equipment for residential needs, golf and turf, and commercial operations such as landscape. Products include the riding lawn tractors sold at dealerships and Home Depot stores nationwide, ranging from the 100 Series to the top of the line X Series; walk-behind mowers; golf course equipment; Gator utility vehicles; landscape and irrigation equipment, and other outdoor power products. This division is experiencing growth as the company expands in the consumer retail market.

Net sales in Commercial and Consumer Equipment were more than $3.7 billion in 2004.

Construction and Forestry Equipment—John Deere originally began selling commercial construction-type equipment in the 1920s. The company's second largest division did not become a separate entity until 1958. Serving contractors, rental companies, municipalities, loggers, and forestry specialists, John Deere Construction and Forestry Equipment is known for its quality in equipment used to harvest and handle timber, including log skidders; feller bunchers; loaders; forwarders; harvesters; and related attachments. The company is also a leading provider of value and quality in construction equipment used to move dirt and materials on construction sites, including backhoe loaders; crawler dozers and loaders; excavators; motor graders; articulated dump trucks; and landscape loaders. The division generated more than $4.2 billion in 2004 sales.

John Deere Credit—Established in 1958, John Deere Credit primarily supports customers and dealers across all company lines of business. This division provides financing for sales and leases of new and used equipment across all manufacturing divisions of the company. John Deere Credit also provides wholesale financing of equipment to dealers and operating loans and retail revolving charge accounts. The division has expanded in recent years to offer more full-service financing to many agricultural clients as well. John Deere Credit generated almost $1.2 billion in 2004 revenue.

John Deere Health—Established in 1985 to serve John Deere employees as well as employees of other companies in select states (those in the same states John Deere already serves its employees), John Deere Health provides managed care solutions. Known for its ability to deliver quality health care benefits at reasonable costs, John Deere Health serves four states, all of which have John Deere facilities: Illinois, Iowa, Tennessee, and Virginia.

Acknowledgments

WHEN MY OLDEST SON WAS BORN MORE THAN 15 YEARS AGO, one of the earliest gifts he received from his grandfather was a small green, collectible John Deere tractor. Bill Rasco had farmed soil in the Arkansas River delta for almost 30 years at the time, and while he knew in all likelihood his grandchildren would not follow in his footsteps, he did know the value of sharing with them treasures of the trade he so loved. If Bill Rasco could not give his grandchildren the farm, he wanted to at least pass pieces of it along. So while the tractor in the box appeared to be another toy for child's play, it was actually one man's way of passing his heritage from one generation to the next. Bill Rasco died in 1994 while his grandchildren were still young, and even though more than 10 years have passed and some aging memories have faded, his grandchildren have never lost sight of the fact that their grandfather was an American farmer who embraced time-tested values rooted in the land. For that, I am grateful.

There is nothing more important to a writer than a good editor. I am fortunate to have forged with Matthew Holt at Wiley a professional relationship built upon trust and frank dialogue that gives each project we do a better than average chance of success. In the business of publishing, that says a lot. Also at Wiley, the same could be said for publisher Larry Alexander, marketing manager Michelle Patterson, and marketing director Laurie Harting. This team of professionals believes in maximizing the potential of every book they do and spares no energy or resources. They never hesitated on this project, eagerly embracing *The John Deere Way* with enthusiasm and commitment from the first moment it was mentioned. Others at Wiley who played an important role in this book's success are Michael Onorato, publicity manager, and Tamara Hummel, editorial assistant.

The day I decided to write books full time for a living was the same day I contacted Frank Weimann of The Literary Group to be my agent. He said no. To my pleasure, he later changed his mind. As a result, I am represented by one of the best literary agents in the difficult world of publishing. Frank Weimann is a dealmaker, and a good one, but his most important characteristic is one we share: the desire to hit the top every time out. His services, friendship, and support on this project and others are appreciated.

The best companies in the world are the hardest to approach because working with an author is not the easiest task, and one can easily say there is everything to lose. John Deere has built its brand and culture for more than a century and a half. The last thing leadership wants to do is have an author tell the story inaccurately, discoloring years of progress. So when I first called John Deere Public Relations Manager Ken Golden, he asked a lot of questions. But the more we talked, the more he understood the need for this project, helping others understand John Deere's unique values-based business and culture that has endured for so long. His assistance for many months has been invaluable. He took valuable time to help me gain access to important people and information, making my calls or help top priority. I will always be grateful for his knowledge of the company, desire to get it right, and willingness to help.

Also at John Deere, a special thank-you to Curtis Linke, who uniquely understands the value of talking about a good thing, and Neil Dahlstrom, the reference archivist for John Deere, who is an accomplished author and historian. Others at John Deere who helped this project along the way are communications manager Mary Leonard and the corporate archivist Vicki Eller.

The Quad Cities area is different from most other metropolitan areas with 400,000 or more residents because with four towns in two different states, split geographically in half by the Mississippi River, there is not one single dominant area. Each flows with relative grace from one to the other so that if you travel from Moline, Illinois, to Davenport, Iowa, or from Bettendorf, Iowa, to Rock Island, Illinois, you hardly know the difference. The benefits are that considering the population base, traffic congestion is rarely a factor and residents speak to one another with small town congeniality. The flip side of that is, of course, that with a small town feel come many small town amenities. I was fortunate, though, to find a few restaurants and havens that served me well time and time again during my extended stay in the Quad Cities.

Special thanks to manager Jack Viviani and the staff of Johnny's Italian Steakhouse (owned by Moline-based Heart of America), located at the John Deere Pavilion. The food was always good and the conversation always ended up somehow on John Deere and its role in the community and in the world. Another Heart of America gem is the Machine Shed, located in Davenport. Other favorite restaurants that gave me something to look forward to when in town included Le Mekong in Moline and Centro in Davenport.

Outside of books, most information compiled by the author was obtained firsthand through interviews or in the John Deere archives. The company has one of the most extensive collections of historical material in the world and recognizes the value of preserving and learning from its history. For the author, these deep resources, including internal communications and advertising materials dating back more than 100 years, make the job of understanding the company and its roots much easier. Additionally, some articles about John Deere or related to its products or leadership were viewed and helpful, most notably "Deere & Company: Sustaining Value" (Harvard Business Review, 1998), and many internal John Deere publications, including the *John Deere Journal*, were most helpful.

Notes

It is not possible to write about John Deere without first mentioning *John Deere's Company: A History of Deere and Company and Its Times* by Wayne G. Broehl Jr. (Doubleday, 1984). While *The John Deere Way* is a contemporary project, drawing on lessons learned from the company's history rather than trying to define the company by its history, Broehl's work remained a valuable resource throughout. It was six years in the making and he left few, if any, stones unturned in the massive work. The book stands among some of the best corporate biographies ever done because of its detail and thoroughness. Even though rarely quoted here, it was a primary source in understanding the founder and the early days of the company.

Another work that must be mentioned in the same breath is *The John Deere Story*, the forthcoming biography of John and Charles Deere to be published in 2005 by the Northern Illinois University Press that is written by Neil Dahlstrom, the reference archivist for John Deere (mentioned in the acknowledgments). Anyone studying the history of the company should refer to his biography of John and Charles Deere, certainly the most complete work ever done on the founder and his son.

Other books that deserve mention include *John Deere Tractors: The First Generation of Power* (Motorbooks International, 2004) by Holly L. Bollinger and *John Deere: A Photographic History* (Motorbooks, 1995) by Robert N. Pripps. These mostly-photographic works provide visual histories of the company that define much of the agricultural landscape in America. In addition, the John Deere-produced book *Genuine Value* (2000) is of the highest quality and worth reading by anyone interested in or studying the company.

Index